D1030033

that's at once more productive and more fulfilling. Read this book to live in a way today that will help you thrive tomorrow."

—DANIEL H. PINK, *New York Times* bestselling author of
When, Drive, and *To Sell Is Human*

"Carey Nieuwhof is about to make a lot of workplaces and leaders healthier with the strategies in *At Your Best.* If you're ready to get your life and leadership back, this book is for you."

—PATRICK LENCIONI, founder of the Table Group and bestselling author of
The Five Dysfunctions of a Team and *The Advantage*

"*At Your Best* is the consummate guide for how to lead yourself well. I can't recommend it highly enough."

—NONA JONES, head of faith-based partnerships for Facebook and
bestselling author of *Success from the Inside Out*
and *From Social Media to Social Ministry*

"With raw transparency and game-changing leadership insights, Carey will empower you to assess your own situation and create a more balanced, intentional, and effective strategy for your life and leadership. Grab a copy for you and everyone on your team."

—CRAIG GROESCHEL, pastor of Life.Church and
New York Times bestselling author

"In *At Your Best,* Carey Nieuwhof offers some of the best strategies I've seen to combat the fatigue, numbness, and overwhelm that mark far too much of life and leadership today. If you're done with being tired and want to accomplish more, this book is exactly what you need."

—ANDY STANLEY, founder and senior pastor of North Point Ministries

"Life balance is impossible to find, but Carey certainly outlines in *At Your Best* a route and a way for all of us, no matter where we are leading, to create margin, live on purpose, rest, and succeed."

—ANNIE F. DOWNS, *New York Times* bestselling author of *That Sounds Fun*

"As prophetic as it is practical, this book is intelligent, well informed, grounded in reality, yet still hugely aspirational. My heart sang as I read it. We don't have to keep living the same broken patterns of overwork, chronic stress, and constant exhaustion. There is another way. A way to both communion and contribution."

—JOHN MARK COMER, founding pastor of Bridgetown Church
and author of *The Ruthless Elimination of Hurry*

"Some books are good reads. Others change your life. *At Your Best* is both. Stress and anxiety are epidemics in our culture. I've seen Carey battle against these to thrive in his own life. With this book, he's going to help you do the same."

—SAM COLLIER, lead pastor of Hillsong Atlanta
and author of *A Greater Story*

"This book is practical, insightful, and incredibly timely! Carey offers us well-researched information with specific tools, tried and tested in his own life, giving us all a chance to lead as our best selves!"

—DANIELLE STRICKLAND, advocate and author of *Better Together*

AT YOUR BEST

AT WOLF'S FEST

AT YOUR BEST

*How to Get
Time, Energy, and Priorities
Working in Your Favor*

CAREY NIEUWHOF

WATERBROOK

AT YOUR BEST

Details in some anecdotes and stories have been changed to protect the identities of the persons involved.

Published in the United States by WaterBrook, an imprint of Random House, a division of Penguin Random House LLC.

WATERBROOK® and its deer colophon are registered trademarks of Penguin Random House LLC.

Library of Congress Cataloging-in-Publication Data
Names: Nieuwhof, Carey, author.
Title: At your best : how to get time, energy, and priorities working in your favor / Carey Nieuwhof.
Description: First edition. | Colorado Springs : WaterBrook, an imprint of Random House, a division of Penguin Random House LLC., [2021] | Includes bibliographical references.
Identifiers: LCCN 2020051292 | ISBN 9780735291362 (hardcover : acid-free paper) | ISBN 9780735291379 (ebook)
Subjects: LCSH: Success—Religious aspects—Christianity. | Time management—Religious aspects—Christianity. | Conflict management—Religious aspects—Christianity.
Classification: LCC BV4598.3 .N54 2021 | DDC 248.4—dc23
LC record available at https://lccn.loc.gov/2020051292

PRINTED IN THE UNITED STATES OF AMERICA ON ACID-FREE PAPER

waterbrookmultnomah.com

2 4 6 8 9 7 5 3

Interior illustrations by Anita Hintz.

SPECIAL SALES Most WaterBrook books are available at special quantity discounts when purchased in bulk by corporations, organizations, and special-interest groups. Custom imprinting or excerpting can also be done to fit special needs. For information, please email specialmarketscms@penguinrandomhouse.com.

To my grandparents Gerrit and Grita Nap,
who had all the time in the world for me

CONTENTS

INTRODUCTION   xiii

PART ONE: THIS MUCH STRESS IS NOT OKAY

1. Build a Life You Don't Want to Escape From
*Why Most of Us Secretly Resent the Life and Career We've
So Carefully Built*   3

2. No More Crazy Busy Life
Live in a Way Today That Will Help You Thrive Tomorrow   22

PART TWO: FOCUS YOUR TIME

3. You Actually Do Have the Time
Two Critical Mental Shifts About Time   43

4. Find Your Green Zone
How to Uncover When You're at Your Best   58

PART THREE: LEVERAGE YOUR ENERGY

5. Do What You're Best At
Investing Your Energy for the Highest Returns   **77**

6. Yellow Zone, Red Zone, and Other Real-Life Problems
How to Leverage Non-Optimal Times and Situations   **94**

PART FOUR: REALIZE YOUR PRIORITIES

7. Hijacked
Why It's So Easy to Fall Perpetually Behind   **111**

8. Distraction-Free
How to Stop Interrupting Yourself   **131**

9. What About People?
*What to Do When the Wrong People Want Your Attention
and the Right People Don't*   **146**

PART FIVE: THEORY, MEET REAL LIFE

10. The Big Sync
How to Synchronize Your Time, Energy, and Priorities Every Day   **169**

11. Thrive On
*How to Recalibrate When Life Blows Up Your
Perfectly Crafted Plan*   **187**

12. Hello from the Future You
It's Not Just What You Accomplish; It's Who You're Becoming   **204**

ACKNOWLEDGMENTS   **211**

GLOSSARY   **215**

NOTES   **217**

INTRODUCTION

I have no idea how you're doing as you pick up this book and start reading, but I'm going to guess you're stressed. That's a pretty accurate diagnosis these days because, well, who isn't stressed?

You and I live with time pressures our great-grandparents couldn't have imagined. Yes, they had pressures too. Crop yields, droughts, and early frosts that threatened the harvest. Or the tyranny and backbreaking conditions of factory life. But my stress—and perhaps yours—is a little different.

For those of us who might call ourselves knowledge workers—entrepreneurs, teachers, engineers, software developers, physicians, nurses, managers, graphic designers, administrators, accountants, pastors, social workers, analysts, attorneys, leaders, or highly motivated stay-at-home parents with dreams—our challenges feel real but are usually hard to diagnose. It's hard to figure out what's making us so stressed.

Here's the truth: you deserve to stop living at an unsustainable pace. What if—instead—you learned how to live at your best, personally and professionally?

That's what this book is about.

I hope it provides both a reasonable diagnosis for you and some welcome relief. I also hope it makes you stop feeling guilty. I'm guessing that, unlike your ancestors' difficulties, most of your problems stem from having too much, not too little. Too many demands. Too many opportunities. Too much information. Too many distractions. Too many choices. Too many people vying for attention. And way too much stuff on the calendar.

I get it. It got to be so much for me that, back in 2006, the overwhelm, overcommitment, and overwork almost took me out. As I touch on in this book, I burned out that year. At first I thought that's what this book was going to be about—my journey into burnout and how to fight back. But books take on a life of their own, and instead, what I've written is far more about the cure than the problem.

My friend Jon, a *New York Times* bestselling author and highly sought-after speaker, once asked me this question: "So, do you have to burn out? Is it just a rite of passage that every leader has to go through? Can't you write a life story where there's no burnout chapter?" Jon was in his late thirties when he asked me that question, just a few years younger than I was when I burned out back in '06. Jon's also a devoted husband and father of two teenage girls.

He asked a relevant question. According to a study of 7,500 full-time American employees, more than 70 percent of adults in their twenties and thirties are experiencing at least some level of burnout.[1] That means a stunning number of young adults are feeling worn out from work and life before they hit their fortieth birthday.

Recently I delivered a keynote talk to leaders in Dallas. The conference host thought it would be a good idea to do an instant poll of the eight hundred leaders in the room to see how many people identified with burnout symptoms. The question was simple: "In your view, over the last year, how many times have you experienced burnout symptoms?"

- never
- once or twice
- regularly (three to six times)
- constantly

While the poll was not scientific, the results stopped me in my tracks. Of the eight hundred leaders gathered, *93 percent* identified as having wrestled through some degree of burnout in the last year. Only 7 percent answered "Never."

When I saw the live results appear on the screen, I had to stop talking. I choked up.

Maybe you're one of the 93 percent.

Or maybe you're one of the 7 percent like Jon who would say, "Not me . . . and I really don't want to end up there."

Which brings us back to Jon's question: *Is burnout inevitable?* I didn't have a good answer when he asked that a few years ago. I have a better one now.

No, Jon, you don't have to burn out. It's not inevitable. And if you're one of the 93 percent, you don't need to stay there. I didn't, and you don't have to either.

That said, stress and its popular cousin, burnout, are spreading like an epidemic. And, like other diseases, sometimes you have it without even realizing what's going on. Maybe you picked up this book (or had it given to you) but thought, *I'm stressed out, but no way I'm* burned *out*. You're perpetually tired, a bit numb, and continually overwhelmed, but you just call it normal because, well, all that feels so normal these days.

So, this isn't a burnout book. It is, instead, a stay-out-of-burnout book.

Things are so different for me now than they were when I burned out. The world is actually a little busier, crazier, and more complicated than it was back in 2006. But inside me, there's a deeper peace, a greater sense of joy, and a way of dealing with the constantly escalating demands of life and leadership that have resulted in my being able to get far more accomplished in far less time. This book is designed to help you find that peace, joy, and much higher productivity too.

One final note before we get started. You'll soon discover (if you haven't already) that I'm a person of faith, and in addition to working briefly in law and now running a leadership company full time, I served as the pastor of a local church for two decades. If that's not anything like your background, don't let it throw you off.

While my life and approach to leadership are fueled by my faith, I've intentionally written this book so that the principles work regardless of your faith perspective. Because so many people need hope. And so many people need help.

I hope this framework provides some practical, powerful strategies for you that will help you for decades to come.

It's time to take your life and leadership back. You ready?

PART 1

THIS MUCH STRESS IS NOT OKAY

BUILD A LIFE YOU DON'T WANT TO ESCAPE FROM

Why Most of Us Secretly Resent the Life and Career We've So Carefully Built

What we call our despair is often only the painful eagerness of unfed hope.

—George Eliot

A decade and a half ago, life seemed to be way more than what I had signed up for and could handle. The organization I was leading had grown bigger than I ever expected it to, and the pressures of leading a staff, handling growth, being married for over a decade, and raising two young sons were more than I had bargained for.

After I pulled into the driveway at home one evening, I sat in the car, the sun having disappeared just long enough that it was neither day nor night. It was gray. I was listening to the radio but not really listening. In my mind, I was grappling with whether I had the energy to walk through the door.

I'm guessing dinner won't be ready. Everything's probably running behind again.

The moment I walk in and decide to lie down on the couch to recharge, not only will I get the eye roll from Toni ("Carey, how can you be this tired again, and can't you see I need your help?"), but I'll also have two kids who bounce over to me, wanting to play.

Homework isn't done—that's for sure. The last thing I feel like doing is helping with homework. Especially math.

Then I wondered, *Has anyone seen me yet? I haven't seen anyone pass by the front window.*

Maybe I should put the car in reverse and head back to work.

Ugh.

As soon as my mind went there, I realized that was no solution. There were just as many issues to deal with at the office—probably more. So, nope, not work.

Maybe swing by Andrew's place?

Wait. I haven't texted him in . . . oh man, a month, six weeks. That won't work.

How is any of this going to get any better? How can I get out of this?

I need to escape.

I can't tell you how many times in that season I wanted to get away. Maybe not escape for real, as in quit my job, take a massive pay cut, destroy my career, and make my wife think (again) that she had made a horrible mistake, but break free in some way. Like a five-year-old who decides he's had enough of his family, packs a spare T-shirt and bandanna in a backpack, and storms off down the street.

The weird thing was that, in my case, everything was going exceptionally well, at least from the outside looking in. I had married my college sweetheart, and we had two healthy sons. Careerwise, I had moved from radio to law to, of all things, pastoring a local church (yes, I know, a career path most high school guidance counselors highly recommend). What I thought would be an eighteen-month assignment in small rural churches ended up turning into decades with the same people in a Toronto-area multisite congregation. By the end of my first decade there, we had become the fastest-growing church in our denomination and one of the larger ones in the country.

So . . . success, right? Well, on many fronts, yes. Except inside me the pressure kept intensifying. I didn't really know how to lead a growing team. I pretended I did, but my strategy of making it up as I went along was wearing thin (mostly on other people).

I was also overrun by the number of people who were by then attending our church. Memorizing names (which at one point I had been really good at) had become an exercise in futility as my brain constantly tripped into overload.

"So good to see you here. You must be new? What's your name again?"

"It's Dave. Same name as last week and when we met the week before."

"Right . . . Dave."

Yes, that actually happened, and who wants a pastor who doesn't remember your name?

My formula for handling growth was as simple as it was stupid: more people equals more hours. As a result, I was cheating sleep, which made me feel simultaneously comatose and irritable most days. I had no insight into how to lead anything bigger, if the growth continued, other than to work harder, which I was beginning to sense would send me over some kind of cliff to an early demise. I'd had quite a bit of optimism earlier in my leadership, but recently I'd started to wonder, *Am I enough?*

My inability to keep up at work also meant I was starting to fail at home. My family rarely got the best of me. Something as small as stepping on a Lego piece in bare feet could lead to a meltdown that lasted all day.

These are just a few snapshots of my life at the time. It all felt so unsustainable. If things got any more complicated or any busier, I was going to go the way of a cheese puff in a windstorm.

Worse, I wasn't even forty yet. *Please don't tell me there are decades more of this ahead!*

Which leads us back to the escape thing. It wasn't a hammock in Fiji that I kept thinking about or an alternate life in some new city with better coffee shops. No, I wanted to escape to a warehouse.

Unlike my current day job, the warehouse offered *so many* attractive features. Managing cardboard boxes would be much simpler than managing the challenges of leadership. Unloading a pallet had so much more appeal than having yet another person unload on me in my office. And the best thing about working in a warehouse is that when you stack boxes, they stay stacked. This being in stark contrast to people, who never seem to do what you want them to do.

It's not like any part of my life was something I didn't want or hadn't helped craft. Yes, life is unpredictable, and no, I couldn't have forecast the details, but I had signed up for all of it, except, of course, for the stress. It's like the life I had so carefully built turned on me, betrayed me. It was nothing like it was supposed to be.

OUT OF TIME, LITTLE ENERGY, NOT GETTING NEARLY ENOUGH DONE

When I was living a life I wanted to escape from, I felt like I never had enough time to get done what really mattered, let alone everything else that was stacked up for me to tackle. My energy level was perpetually low, as though I were toggling between autopilot and the zombie universe. Sometimes it seemed like I was one bad day away from deflating completely. And as far as my priorities went, it was as though I had almost no control over my life, because what I wanted to do got hijacked by other people and commitments on a daily—no, hourly—basis.

I didn't want to screw my life up, but I had a sinking feeling that's precisely what I was doing. I was overwhelmed, overcommitted, and overworked doing exactly what I thought I wanted to do with my life. Equally disheartening was the reality that my dreams were getting squeezed out in the process. I had always wanted to write a book. Prior to age forty, I had typed exactly zero words in pursuit of that dream. My family wasn't hitting our financial goals. To make it worse, I had no hobbies, I never found time to exercise, and I quietly resented people who made the time to enjoy life. I was barely surviving.

Many people are overwhelmed, overcommitted, and overworked doing exactly what they thought they wanted to do with their lives.

Eventually it all caught up with me. In 2006, not only did my unsustainable pace crush me—it also nearly killed me. I slid headlong into burnout. I spent months with my passion gone, my energy sapped, and my hope barely flickering. It wasn't the end, but it definitely felt like it. I was numb. It's like my body went on strike and said, "Enough with the craziness."

If you don't declare a finish line to your work, your body will.

On that note, any idea what chronic stress might be doing to *your* body? Sure, maybe you haven't burned out. But if you don't think that stress costs you anything, you might want to think again.

THE PRICE OF STRESS

Stress—which is medically defined as "any intrinsic or extrinsic stimulus that evokes a biological response"[1]—can apparently do some real damage. The American Psychological Association noted that the impact of stress can include headaches, chronic pain, shortness of breath, and full-on panic attacks. Stress has also been linked to heartburn, acid reflux, bloating, nausea, indigestion, the loss of sexual desire, lower sperm count, lower sperm motility, and the inability to conceive. In addition, stress can adversely affect memory function, slow your reaction time, and create behavioral and mood disorders.

Lovely.

Stress can also impair communication between your immune system and your HPA axis—a complex, multiorgan feedback system that regulates stress hormones, including cortisol. No, I hadn't heard of that either until I looked it up, but apparently, stress raises your cortisol levels, which in turn can spawn a host of physical and mental health issues, like chronic fatigue, diabetes, obesity, depression, and autoimmune disorders. Research also links stress to cardiovascular problems as life threatening as heart attacks and strokes.[2]

This, surprisingly, is only a *partial* list of the damage stress can do, but need we say more? I didn't think so.

Technology only makes this all more complicated. You used to have to go to the office to work. Now, thanks to your phone, the office goes to you—a beautiful gift to all of us who are workaholics. Our inability to control our use of technology is making us sicker, more anxious, and more distraught than ever before.

So, all that said, do you have any idea what your personal stress level is? To help you find out, I designed a short burnout quiz that can give you a rough idea of how high your current stress level is. You can take it for free at www.AtYourBestToday .com. The results, while nonscientific, can give you an idea of what your personal burnout level is.

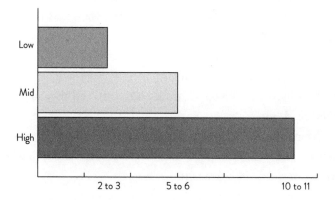

BURNOUT INDICATOR

SURVIVAL IS NOT YOUR GOAL

You didn't sign up for a disease-riddled existence spawned by your lifestyle. Neither did I. Yet practically all of us are overwhelmed, overcommitted, and overworked. Parents feel perpetually behind. Retired people are stressed. So are entry-level employees and high school students, who are increasingly being rattled by anxiety and panic attacks. Meanwhile, entrepreneurs, midlevel managers, nurses, lawyers, tradespeople, first responders, accountants, church leaders, and even the medical doctors who diagnose our stress find themselves deluged just trying to keep up with everything.

Which is really quite remarkable. After all, how did the most prosperous people who ever lived (which is everyone in the developed world in the twenty-first century) make their lives about *survival?* Seriously. I mean, you and I hardly have to make our own loincloths or hunt deer in the forest to feed our families. There is little about your life or mine that requires us to merely *survive,* but in the midst of being the most affluent and free people who ever lived, we've enslaved ourselves to survival.

How on earth did we get to the place where we say things like the following?

"I just need to make it to summer vacation."

"Let me survive final exams."

"Really, my goal is to get through to July, and then all will be good . . . I hope."

Many of us have found ourselves in a place we didn't want to be: resenting the life and career we've so carefully built. Or if we're not there yet, we're getting close.

So, let me ask *you:* Are you eager to escape? Is your life filled with activity on the outside and emotional emptiness on the inside?

The first thing to do is face up to the reality.

IT'S NOT JUST A SEASON

To revive some semblance of hope amid all the overwhelm, maybe you tell yourself that the stress you're feeling and the crazy busy life you're living is fine because it's *just a season.*

I spent the first decade of my time in leadership convincing myself that I was just in a busy period. It seemed like a plausible explanation. After all, I was carrying so much. So I would tell my friends and family, "Yeah, it's crazy now, but it's just a busy season."

When I'd see them a month later, we'd repeat the whole conversation.

Eventually my friends and family started mocking me, as only friends and family do. "You're always in a busy season. That's what you say every single time. Ha!"

They were right.

Their honesty made me finally get honest with myself. My repeated explanations of the *new* thing that was making life crazy—and how everything would be better once the project/trip/holiday/year was over—made me sound like a guy who hadn't taken the time to listen to his futile little script in a while.

Don't use the same excuse I did. Seasons, after all, have beginnings and endings. If your busy season has no ending, *it's not a season—it's your life.*

I'm not trying to bring you down. I'm trying to help you out. Maybe it's time to tell yourself the truth about what's been happening in your life.

To help you see it in a fresh light, let me put a twist on this. What might you say to the generation coming after you if you were *absolutely truthful* about what you've discovered life is *really* like? Would you say something like, well, this?

THE MOST HONEST COMMENCEMENT SPEECH EVER

Imagine yourself stepping up to a podium to deliver your first commencement address and telling a college graduating class something like this:

"I am honored to be with you today at your commencement from one of the finest universities in the world. Most people, in a moment like this, try to inspire you. I'm here to inform you because, kids, the truth is your friend.

"You're likely wondering what's ahead. Let me give you a snapshot.

"To begin with, most of you are in debt beyond any comfortable level. Good luck paying that back, but here's a sneak peak of the future you've financed. If you aren't already in love, maybe you'll find someone soon and settle down. You'll get a job—hopefully a career job, if you're that lucky. At some point, if you're so inclined, you may even have kids. But underneath, there will be undiagnosed pain—an unspoken sense that there's a meaningful calling for you but your life is spinning out of control and you can't even pause long enough to discover why. As you sit in an office day after day, slowly suffocating, you'll live with this angst of never coming close to what you suspect you might have been. You won't fully understand the anxiety, of course, but it will eventually dawn on you that this life you'd anticipated for so long is one that, most days, you long to escape.

"For some of you, the escape will happen every day at four o'clock or five or nine—whenever you can finally head home or close the laptop for good. You'll end up binge-watching your favorite show over takeout because you're too tired to cook or scrolling social media until your eyes sting and you fall asleep, phone still in hand. Some of you will find your escape in a third glass of bourbon or wine most nights, or you'll unwind with a joint or another trip to the fridge because reality feels a little too heavy to carry. For still others among you, it will be the prescription medication you're no longer taking as directed, or you'll find yourself drifting away from the people closest to you and flirting online with people you used to know in high school, because your current relationship is oh-so-dull (despite what your Instagram feed suggests). Or maybe you'll live for the weekend. Or your next vacation. Or the lake. Or the game. Or the pool. Or your next massage. Anything but what you're doing right now.

"Some of you will bury your pain with, ironically, more work. Workaholism is, after all, the most rewarded addiction in the nation. You can be fired for drinking too much, but working too much usually gets you promoted. It also gets you a raise. So you dump yourself into bed exhausted most nights, only to do it all again tomorrow.

"Finally, a small number of you won't lapse into any of those patterns. Instead, you'll soldier on and endure four decades of banality to achieve the dream of having a decent life when you retire, assuming you live that long.

"All this and more awaits you, my friends. Welcome to life as we know it."

Well, how's that for distressing?

As dismal as it is to read it in black and white, that's the script an inordinate number of highly "successful" people adopt. Most of us have embraced some version of it. I did. You probably have.

So, here we are as a culture.

Busy is the default.

Slammed is normal.

Crazy time is all the time.

Life has been reduced to going through the motions.

Bottom line? This much stress is reality—and it is not okay.

Here's the good news. You don't have to live a life that stresses you out every day. Just because this is your life now doesn't mean this has to be your life forever. It wasn't for me, and it won't be for you either.

BURN THE SCRIPT

The script that passes for normal life for millions of people has got to go. I'd love for you to decide today that you're going to tear it up. On second thought, go further. Burn it. Get a can of gas, throw a match on it, and watch the last ember drift off into space. That's what I did.

On the other side of my burnout, I was determined to live in a fundamentally different way. I had no idea how to do that, so I spent the next few years reading widely and hiring coaches and counselors to help me figure out how to live in a whole new way. I was tired of feeling like I was always out of time, sick of dragging my feet through day after endless day, and more than done with putting in an eight- or ten-hour day and feeling like I had accomplished everything for everyone else and nothing on my own to-do list, despite giving it my best shot. If that's what normal was, I was done.

I had a choice to make. Instead of heading to a warehouse or hammock or abandoning everything I'd built over my life to date, I decided to change the one thing I could change: *me.*

I rebuilt my life. My family didn't change; I stayed married to the same woman and committed to our two sons. I kept the same job (not saying you have to, because it's not a prerequisite for transformational change). We didn't even leave town. I just changed what I was doing with my days and how I was doing it.

As I studied top performers, I realized they moved way past

manage energy

time management and were highly focused on managing not just their time but their energy. Usually they had one thing in common: *they did what they were best at when they were at their best.* In other words, they worked in their area of principal gifting and passion when their energy was at its highest during the day. And as a result, they got their top priorities accomplished day in and day out. I started to implement that rhythm in my own life as a keystone habit. *Keystone habit*

So, while not much on the outside changed, *I* started to change—for the better. I got my life back and my leadership back. Learning how to better use my resources also proved surprisingly effective in restoring my heart, defeating my cynicism, and giving me back a joy in living that I'd thought was gone forever.

Let me get specific. After I started doing what I was best at when I was at my best, I

- saw our congregation grow to three times the size it was before I burned out
- worked through the funk in my marriage to find a place where my wife and I felt genuinely in love again
- published five books in eleven years
- launched a leadership podcast and started a blog that now reaches millions of leaders a year
- traveled about a hundred days a year, speaking around the world and investing in leaders
- started a company that produces resources that help people thrive in life and leadership
- discovered three hobbies I love
- began exercising
- lost twenty pounds

- started getting a full night's sleep pretty much every night
- enjoyed more time off than I ever had in my adult life
- spent more time with my family than ever while being more effective at work

At the time, I had no idea how well the changes I made would set me up for the digital revolution of smartphones, social media, and 24-7 access that was right around the corner, as well as the rapid growth of my own leadership that would soon follow, but the transformation was pivotal to helping me thrive during the coming deluge.

All this might sound a little over the top, but the best part is that similar things have been happening in the lives of thousands of other people whom I've had the privilege of teaching as they've adopted the principles we'll cover. Doing what you're best at when you're at your best unlocks potential and freedom on a scale that shocks a lot of people who try it. It has the potential to change everything.

GET EVERYTHING THAT'S WORKING *AGAINST* YOU WORKING *FOR* YOU

As I've already hinted, if you look at how you navigate your life, regardless of where you are, what you do, or whom you do it with, you deal with three primary assets: time, energy, and priorities. Whether you're writing your last college exam, launching your company, landing an account, spending the day off site with your team, waking up on your day off, getting the kids' lunches packed, or even taking a vacation at the beach, every day you fight for how your time, energy, and priorities are spent. Practically speaking, you face a thousand little questions every day:

- *Will the website be live in time for the launch?*
- *How much more effort should I put into trying to persuade this person to come on board?*
- *Will I ever be able to get my email inbox to zero, or should I just stop trying?*
- *How much caffeine will I need to tackle the final session of the day and then entertain everyone who came in from out of town?*
- *Should I interview the new hire tomorrow morning or wait until the afternoon so I can get my work done first?*
- *Do I really have time for a round of golf before my daughter's dance lesson?*
- *Am I going to do a little more research for that final term paper or go out with my friends?*
- *Will I head to the beach today or slip into town to explore a nearby village?*

For years, it felt like time, energy, and priorities were working *against* me. When you don't have an intentional strategy for how to manage those three assets, that's exactly what happens. But I've been living a whole different way for a decade and a half now, and I want to help you learn to make the most of your own time, energy, and priorities.

What if you could control your calendar and learn how to say no without the threat of losing friends or influence?

What if you could become much better at what you do while working fewer hours?

What if you could protect your time, prioritize your family, and still crush it at work?

Applying what they've learned from the *At Your Best* principles, the people below have achieved beautiful results (all true stories):

- Jeff and Al charted the energy levels of their eighty-member staff and reorganized their meeting schedules to raise productivity and deepen employee engagement.
- Christina discovered "insane levels of productivity" to develop a phone app, work out, and spend more time with her newborn.
- John lost seventy pounds by making time for eating healthier, exercising, and getting a full night's sleep. He also built a deck on his house, started hiking, and took up a hobby.
- Steven started a blog—something he'd wanted to do for a long time.
- Cassi became significantly less stressed and more present with her kids while at the same time starting a blog, getting more active on social media, and writing her first book proposal that she's pitching to publishers.
- Andrew started taking a full day off every week for the first time.
- Dave, a pastor and the father of two kids under the age of four, used the extra hours he freed up to be home far more often with his family and to master how to speak without using notes.
- Zach began his doctorate.
- Joel, the executive director of a nonprofit that helps students, moved from being in twelve schools to being in twenty-nine within four months, nearly doubling the number of students helped from 800 to 1,500.

Constant stress denies so many people permission to dream or to accomplish what they're called to do. What most people have discovered when they apply the principles we'll cover is that there is a much better way to live than barely making it through the day, only to get up and repeat the drudgery tomorrow.

WHAT'S YOUR DREAM?

I love asking people what their dreams are.

Sometimes the dreams feel big. Entrepreneurs cast vision about the new idea that they're struggling to get off the ground amid a million obstacles. CEOs tell me how much they long to find an alternative to the incessant pressure. I've talked to so many people who want to write a book or launch a podcast but just can't find the bandwidth to pull it off.

Sometimes the dreams are so simple they make me smile, because all of us have beautiful things and people who somewhere along the line got squeezed out of our lives. One woman told me that what she really wanted was a weed-free garden—her plants used to be so life giving to her. Another told me she used to paint watercolors and would love to get back the spark that painting created in her life. Fathers tell me they miss seeing their kids' games and they're done with showing up late for school plays. Mothers tell me they're tired of being disengaged from the kids they love and sick of feeling like they can't give their kids what they really need. Others tell me they just want an actual day off with zero interruptions for once.

You probably have a dream—or maybe even a calling—that went into hiding long ago or seems so impossible that you're afraid to say it out loud or even admit it to yourself. In this journey ahead, you're going to get space to dream again and learn the strategy that will free up the time to pursue that dream.

I don't know what your goals and dreams are or what your calling in life is, but I do know it's possible not only to become de-stressed and to avoid burnout and to come back from it but also to *thrive*. To live fully alive. I would love for you to pull yourself out of the soul-sucking bog that passes for existence—the job you can never get ahead on, the dreams you let die, the soul you've neglected, the endless social media scroll that makes you envious, angry, and vacuous all at once, the numbness you've allowed yourself to believe is normal—and embrace an approach that will be so much more life giving. To truly be at your best. Not somebody else's best, but yours.

That's what this book is about.

If you stick with it through the next few hours together, you'll see results you may never have thought were possible. And when you're done, you'll have built a life that you no longer want to escape from. Instead, you might actually love it.

CHAPTER 1 IN A SNAP

- The typical formula for growth is as simple as it is stupid: more people equals more hours.

- Many people are overwhelmed, overcommitted, and overworked doing exactly what they thought they wanted to do with their lives.

- If you don't declare a finish line to your work, your body will.

- You used to have to go to the office to work more. Now, thanks to your phone, the office goes to you.

- The most prosperous people who ever lived (which is everyone in the developed world in the twenty-first century) have made their lives about survival.

- Too many people build lives they want to escape from.

- If your busy season has no ending, it's not a season—it's your life.

- Workaholism is the most rewarded addiction in our society.

- Top performers do what they're best at when they're at their best—they work in their area of principal gifting and passion when their energy is at its highest.

- Everybody gets three primary assets every day: time, energy, and priorities.

- When you don't have an intentional strategy, then time, energy, and priorities work against you, not for you.

- You can protect your time, prioritize your family, and still crush it at work.

- Constant stress denies many people permission to dream or to accomplish what they're called to do.

Time, Energy, Prioritie

NO MORE CRAZY BUSY LIFE

Live in a Way Today That Will Help You Thrive Tomorrow

Anxiety is the dizziness of freedom.

—Søren Kierkegaard

If you listen to the advice designed to help people who are overwhelmed and stressed, which is dispensed by friends, advisers, and online gurus, the standard tips for beating your crazy busy life often sound like this: (1) get an adequate amount of sleep each night; (2) engage in regular physical exercise; and (3) maintain health in your most important relationships.

It's all really solid advice.

There are only a few problems with it. First, you already know all that. Second, if that's all it took, you could be in a state of bliss tomorrow. And third, even when practiced, those three therapies barely take the edge off. Even decently rested people who have friends and can bench-press a tiny house are stressed out.

So your struggle continues.

Another regular piece of well-intentioned advice is to take more time off. Make sure, the gurus say, that you get a regular day off each week or take the full weekend. Recharge and renew. Others will add that you should take *all* your vacation time, and if you happen to be one of the lucky ones who gets four weeks of paid vacation, that's a pretty sweet deal. Again, hat tip to people who take their days off. That's a really good idea.

If you work for a *really* progressive company or nonprofit, maybe they'll even give you a sabbatical. Then, once every seven years, you get to leave (probably exhausted) for a few months off, live a temporarily magical life in some villa in the south of France, where you can buy fresh macarons at the patisserie every morning, only to interrupt the bliss to head back into life in the suburbs, where you'll quickly grow resentful of your next seven years.

I've often been puzzled by why sabbaticals, long vacations, proper sleep, and even exercise rarely solve the problems of burnout and feeling perpetually overwhelmed.

Here's why.

Time *off* won't heal you when the problem is how you spend your time *on.* It's ludicrous to think that a few days off here or a few months off there are going to resolve the issues created by a perpetually overwhelming life. Taking a day off or a vacation as a solution to feeling chronically overwhelmed is about as strategic as telling an alcoholic that he should stop drinking on Thursdays.

Plus, this way of thinking ("days off are my answer") leaves you longing to be somewhere else. You'll spend your life working for the weekend. Living for time off is just another form of escaping.

Time off won't heal you when the problem is how you spend your time on.

Days off, vacations, and even sabbaticals aren't a complete solution for an unsustainable pace.

A sustainable pace is the solution for an unsustainable pace.

PATTERN RECOGNITION: SUCKED INTO THE STRESS SPIRAL

You may have seen your story in the first chapter, but underneath your story is a series of patterns that shaped your story. In fact, your life consists of a series of ongoing patterns. I know you probably think you're more creative than that (I like to think I am), but try moving the toothbrush to another drawer, taking a different route home from work, or sitting in a different spot at the dinner table tonight, and you'll see what I mean. Most of us are far more creatures of habit than we realize.

Some of the patterns you're currently repeating have taken you into what I've named the Stress Spiral—a place where you feel perpetually overwhelmed, overcommitted, and overworked. See if you recognize these dynamics.

Unfocused Time

Here's how the Stress Spiral pulls you in and under. You and I get the immense gift of time handed to us every day, but we live like we never have enough of it. One of the key reasons is our failure

our failure to focus time,

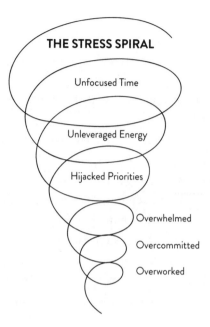

THE STRESS SPIRAL

Unfocused Time

Unleveraged Energy

Hijacked Priorities

Overwhelmed

Overcommitted

Overworked

to focus time. We have a tendency to treat all waking hours as though they were the same, even though they aren't. Think about it: having a conversation with your significant other at 3:00 p.m. is probably a very different experience from having one at 3:00 a.m. Even though you intuitively sense the difference there, if you're like many people, for most of your waking hours you really don't channel your time intentionally.

As a result, you usually do your most important things randomly, squeezing them into leftover slots or sometimes not tackling them at all (like that big meeting you're supposed to be preparing for). You fail to use your most productive hours to do what you're best at. Not focusing your time means you don't intentionally assign specific activities to designated time windows other than, perhaps, deciding to go for lunch at twelve thirty or hit the gym at four. Meetings happen randomly. Interruptions and distractions dominate your unscheduled time, so even when you set aside a few hours to get things done, your time usually gets hijacked. You get frustrated with other people interrupting you and taking up your time, but as you'll see, the reason other people don't value your time is that you don't—or at least you haven't learned to yet.

Consequently, you live with a constant sense of time famine. Your to-do list only seems to expand, and the gnawing sense of scarcity *(There's never enough time!)* keeps growing. Even though you sometimes cheat sleep to try to catch up, you rarely seem to get ahead and feel guilty about working long hours to keep up. Your answer to everything is *try harder* or *get more efficient,* but nothing seems to relieve the tension or solve the problem.

The good news is that having unfocused time is 100 percent fixable. It's just that most people never get there. You will.

Unleveraged Energy

While almost all people caught in the Stress Spiral realize they are competing *with* time and *for* time, few ever pay attention to their energy, other than to complain about having low amounts of it. Which is a shame, because energy—even *low* energy—can be leveraged in a way that is surprisingly helpful.

Unleveraged energy springs from failing to cooperate with your personal energy levels as they rise and fall over the course of the day. Not leveraging your energy means you squander your most productive hours, not because you intend to but because you don't know when they happen or how to schedule your life around them.

When you finally get to your most important tasks or people, you're too tired to engage deeply or are at least far less engaged than you could be. Vocationally, your most important work usually suffers because you don't spend your best energy doing it.

Relationally, your family and your closest coworkers and staff rarely get the best of you.

Hijacked Priorities

The Stress Spiral pulls you in even further when your best intentions get jettisoned because your priorities got hijacked. Hijacked priorities happen when you allow other people to determine what you get done. I know that was a simple sentence, but let me repeat it.

Hijacked priorities happen when you allow other people to determine what you get done.

For people caught in the Stress Spiral, that pretty much describes every day of their lives, including days off. As a result, despite their determination to get ahead, they spend much of their day responding to the daily bombardment of messages, texts, emails, DMs, and other interruptions. This leads them to feeling like they never have bandwidth to get done what they're supposed to do.

People whose priorities get consistently hijacked usually haven't learned how to say no. Often they don't even realize they're *allowed* to say no. Even if they understand that saying no is important, they don't know how to do it in a way that doesn't burn bridges or offend people.

No wonder they're stressed.

Those, in a nutshell, are the patterns you'll find in the lives of people caught in the Stress Spiral. They were my patterns too. The Stress Spiral is so pernicious that falling into it is inevitable unless you know how to resist it with a counterstrategy. Fortunately, there *is* a counterstrategy.

THE THRIVE CYCLE: DOING WHAT YOU'RE BEST AT
WHEN YOU'RE AT YOUR BEST

In the Stress Spiral, almost everything is random because you don't have a strategy. How you spend your time is random. You're not really thinking about your energy levels, so you tackle things in a scattered way, squeezing them in whenever possible. Interruptions and distractions keep you from realizing your priorities. You haven't really thought deeply about what you're best at (like, for real, what are you *best* at?), and you're not sure exactly when you're at your best most days.

Stress has patterns. So does thriving. The opposite of the Stress Spiral is something we'll call the Thrive Cycle. And at the heart of the Thrive Cycle is the habit of doing what you're best at when you're at your best. For me, doing what I'm best at when I'm at my best has been the Archimedes lever that moved my world. It generated all the productivity I shared with you in the last chapter (and more), but better than that, it's resulted in a deeper, lasting peace. That peace comes from, among other things, the assurance of knowing that if I can just do what I'm best at when I'm at my best for a good chunk of each day (as I get time, energy, and priorities working for me), my effectiveness soars—work is far better, and my home life has a quality and joy that was missing for too many years.

The way to be at your best is to focus your time, leverage your energy, and realize your priorities. When those three things work in sync, you move into the Thrive Cycle, a virtuous loop that will carry you far more effectively through the days and decades ahead. Once you start to master the patterns, principles, and strategies in the Thrive Cycle, the result (as you'll soon see) is that dreams get acted on, hope is no longer deferred, and a lot more gets accomplished in less time.

This may come as no surprise, but the strategies in the Thrive Cycle are essentially the opposite of the approaches in the Stress Spiral. Sometimes the key to success really is to do the opposite of what everyone else is doing (like buying when everyone else is selling and selling when everyone else is buying). That's true when it comes to your personal habits, rhythms, and disciplines.

This is just a brief overview of the Thrive Cycle because, well, that's what we're going to spend the rest of the book exploring in detail and applying in real-life ways. So you can grasp the big picture, here's the overview of how to thrive by doing what you're best at when you're at your best and getting time, energy, and priorities moving in your direction.

THE THRIVE CYCLE

Focused
Time

AT YOUR
BEST

Thriving   Leveraged
                        Energy

Realized
Priorities

Focused Time

Rather than spending your time randomly, in the Thrive Cycle you focus your time through several approaches. The first refocus involves an attitude shift in how you *think* about time. The big surprise? You actually have the time to do anything you want to do. And sure, if that sounds a little too positive-mindset woo-woo to you, hang on until chapter 3 where you'll see how real that truth is. Thinking matters. Most people don't think about how to value their time as intentionally as they think about how to value a new pair of shoes (which they probably won't even possess in two years).

There are other adjustments we'll explore about how you handle time, but the biggest shift takes place when you realize that you have only a limited number of highly productive hours in a day. Some hours will produce better results for you than others, and focusing your time means you'll treat those hours differently and, through that, you'll discover much higher levels of productivity than you're used to. Those limited hours during which you're at your best compose something you'll soon come to call your Green Zone. You'll learn how to discover your most productive hours in chapter 4.

Bottom line? Focusing your time will help you get more accomplished in less time.

Leveraged Energy

The real power of the Thrive Cycle happens here, when you learn how to leverage your energy levels that wax and wane over the course of the day.

By default, most people compete with their energy levels, trying to push through low ebbs or even denying that they're struggling in a given moment. Rather than competing with your energy levels, you'll learn to cooperate with them. Leveraging your energy (along with focusing your time) will lead you into the heart of peak productivity, which comes from using your Green Zone hours every day to do what you're best at when you're at your best.

Having accomplished your most important work during your Green Zone, you're then free to do other things as your energy dips to other zones—your Yellow Zone and your Red Zone. As you might guess from the colors yellow and red, these are the zones where your energy is somewhere between average and, well, dismal. And as you'll learn, that's perfectly fine and very natural. You'll start cooperating with those realities, and it will be more liberating than you imagine.

Most people concentrate on managing their time but never think about managing their energy. But leveraging your energy is where you start to see exponential results. When you leverage your energy, you'll realize you're capable of producing not just *more* work but much *better* work than you thought possible.

Realized Priorities

Until now, everything has been fun theory. But this is where the strategies that will help you realize your priorities come in. You'll learn a number of tactics, tips, and tricks that will help you eliminate distractions, learn how to say no, figure out how to handle the complexities of change and growth, and protect your Green Zone every day so you can accomplish more in less time.

At the heart of this is your calendar. To make everything work together seamlessly, you'll start approaching your calendar in a very different way. Adding the discipline of calendaring your energy zones, priorities, and key relationships will move everything you've learned from intention to reality.

As a result, rather than allowing other people, interruptions, and the noise of everyday life to sabotage your priorities, you'll accomplish them. You'll have made time for the things and people that matter most.

. . .

That's the big picture. We'll come back to these basic concepts again and again, and by the time you're finished, all this will feel like a set of shortcuts to a much less stressful life.

A SIMPLE MAXIM THAT SUMMARIZES EVERYTHING

As I learned the strategies I've just introduced to you and will now start to explore in detail, I found myself trying to find a maxim that summed it all up. The mantra I adopted is so simple you might be tempted to dismiss it. But it's one that's guided me now for years and I hope can guide you. "Live in a way today that will help you thrive tomorrow."

When I get all the components of the Thrive Cycle working together, that's what happens. This mantra is also the antithesis of how most people in the Stress Spiral navigate their lives. The Stress Spiral mantra may as well be "Live in a way today that will make you *struggle* tomorrow."

Living in a way today that will help you thrive tomorrow will also become a little scorecard that gives you instant feedback on how sustainable your current pace is. If you're not thriving (that is, tomorrow's going to be a mess), it will remind you to adjust things, and you'll have the tool kit to do that.

Live in a way today that will help you thrive tomorrow.

Before we dive into the details of the Thrive Cycle in the chapters ahead, it's important to define thriving. For me (and for most of the leaders I've trained in this), to really thrive doesn't mean you're succeeding in just one part of your life; it means you're thriving in *all* of it. Driven people often excuse having terrible personal lives because they're winning at work. For too long, I bought that lie. I don't anymore. Winning at work while losing at home means you're losing. Period.

As you apply this maxim, don't just think about work or tasks. Thriving should encompass *all* of life. Trust me—these strategies will help you crush it at work. But please also think people. Think soul. Think purpose. The Thrive Cycle will introduce or reintroduce you to the part of life that matters most: a meaningful existence.

I regularly evaluate whether I'm thriving in five key areas of my life: spiritual, relational, emotional, financial, and physical. Whenever I do that, what results is margin and greater health in all five aspects of life.

REMEMBER MARGIN?

Margin is *space.* It's room to breathe. Margin is so rare in our culture, with every spare minute taken up with something. Technology hasn't helped us much in this respect.

Margin is what you experienced when you were a kid and your six-week summer break felt the way a year (or decade) feels today. It's what you had when you were *sooooo* bored and your mom told you to find something to entertain yourself until dinner but you rolled your eyes at how that felt like forever from now. Margin is when you used your $10 bill to buy all the candy and gum you wanted and you still had $7.14 left over. Margin is the leftovers, the extra, the grace.

Yeah, I know—it's been awhile.

As you master the concepts ahead and think holistically, you'll start to create margin in your calendar, you'll have energy left over at the end of the workday, and you'll have a new system that means other people don't crowd your decision-making. If you're a person of faith, as I am, that will mean time to develop your spirituality through prayer, meditation, reflection, and community.

Creating margin allows you to take time for yourself. You'll take the time to get to know yourself better and work through your stuff—self-awareness and emotional intelligence are some of the greatest predictors of success in leadership and in life, after all. Most people never find the time to grow personally, and that's a shame.

Thriving means better self-care—getting a good night's sleep (and maybe taking naps), eating healthier meals, and heading to the gym, lifting a little, or going out for a run more regularly.

You'll find space to nurture life-giving relationships again, with nights out so enjoyable you lose track of time—you know, the kind of dinner where you think you've been together for one hour but it's been five. (Think of that as payback for meetings where five minutes feels like five hours.) You'll make time for the kinds of moments with friends during which you laugh so hard you cry and your stomach hurts.

Intimacy, after all, is shared experience, and creating a regular rhythm of shared experiences with a handful of close friends and family members will help you thrive. Because you are so much more productive at work and have healthier boundaries, you'll free up far more time for this joy.

Finally, thriving means creating margin in your finances too. Often the reason people struggle financially is they don't devote the time they need to really come to grips with their situation. You and I have both heard of people who make $300,000 a year but have a load of debt. We also know people who make only $30,000 a year but have money in the bank. Margin has less to do with income than it does with healthy habits. I've lived with financial margin and I've lived without it. I promise you that living with it is far better. If you haven't done so yet, you'll carve out time to develop better habits.

One of my favorite things about the kind of margin that comes from living in a way today that will help me thrive tomorrow is that it makes me nicer. Get me on a slammed day, and it's so easy for me to snap at you. Get me when I feel like I have a wealth of time, and I'll smile, pull up a chair, and invite you to hang out. I am the most kind when I have the most margin. So, I'll guess, are you.

WILL EVERY DAY BE PERFECT?

The advantages of doing what you're best at when you're at your best sound pretty awesome, don't they? "Will every day be perfect, Carey?" you ask. "Will we spend every Tuesday afternoon in hammocks, sipping cold drinks?"

Fortunately for me, yes, that's exactly what my life looks like. Every day *is* perfect.

Okay, that's a *complete lie.*

Nope, every day will not be perfect. Just ask my wife. My kids. My staff. My friends.

Do I screw up? Yep. I do.

The challenge—my challenge—is that life isn't static and I'm far from faultless. You can do everything we talk about in this book—finally get time, energy, and priorities working for you, master your new Thrive Calendar, crush your goals—and, two months later, hit a snag. Your organization grew again (or declined). You joined a new social media channel and found a new distraction that sucked up the day. You moved into a new house or to a new city and changed jobs. Or maybe, because you're human like me, you forgot the strategy for a while and slipped back into old habits. Or perhaps you simply found yourself with a new set of stressors, like a neighbor who enjoys blasting heavy metal.

As you know, life changes every day.

But the good news is that everything you'll learn here can be reworked for your new reality. Got a new job? You can adjust. Got a promotion? You'll figure out how to thrive again. Picked up an enjoyable hobby? You can find time for that. Just found out you're pregnant with triplets? Okay, maybe the strategy can't solve everything.

Later in the book, I have a full chapter on how to recalibrate when life throws you curveballs. And as you know, life throws more than a few.

Every day is not perfect, but the trajectory is forward and upward. The Thrive Cycle has led thousands of people into far more productive and effective lives with meaningfully reduced stress levels. That's what it's done for me since 2006. That was a long time ago, yet using the strategy you're about to learn, I've stayed out of burnout ever since and I've been able to greatly increase my capacity while reducing the hours I work. I get way more done in far less time, and I get the most important things done.

What you'll discover is that when you adopt the strategy as a framework, it can scale up or down with you. It flexes. That's why it's worked for CEOs of eight-figure companies and for college students trying to pass their final exams. That's why, all these years later, I'm even more in love with it than I was when I adopted it. It's kept me sane, breathing, and thriving. For many of us now, it's been undeniably, quantifiably rewarding.

UP TO A THOUSAND MORE PRODUCTIVE HOURS

I've got a pretty sweet promise for you. When you start doing what you're best at when you're at your best, there's a solid chance you can gain three productive hours *each day*. That's right. Three hours daily.

When you extrapolate that, it gets liberating quickly. Three productive hours a day equals 1,095 reclaimed hours over the course of a year.

Imagine what you could do with the thousand hours you get back over the next year (and the years that follow). Professionally, you might launch your own company, write that book you've been meaning to write, open some new locations, or solve the problem you haven't even been able to think about. Personally, you could tuck your kids into bed at night, actually take weekends off, develop a hobby, read more books, or buff up like you've been meaning to.

Because individual mileage varies, let's say you don't realize three freed-up hours a day (for example, you're already super efficient). I'm still confident the strategies can help you free up at least three productive hours each *week*. That may not sound like much, but do the math. Three hours a week of newly productive time becomes 156 hours a year. And guess what that is? That's the equivalent of *almost four weeks of vacation*. You get a month of newly freed-up, "do what you want with it" time. Personally, I'd sign up for that.

Most people I've led through the strategy free up a minimum of three hours a week. Some really do free up three hours a *day*. The latter has been my story.

I can't wait until we get to the Thrive Calendar, where I'll teach you how to schedule time for what you really want to do in life.

OVERWHELMED, OVERCOMMITTED, AND OVERWORKED NO MORE

With all these advantages in mind and a solid, proven strategy ahead, let me ask, Are you tired of telling the people you love most to wait while you try to hack your way through your daily to-do list or while you make "just one more" call? Maybe you want to not only stay married but actually enjoy your relationship again. You're tired of the hectic, harried life that's made your relationship feel transactional and a ghost of what it used to be.

Now that you understand how you and I got into the Stress Spiral (and why most people stay stuck there), it's time to escape—this time in a really positive direction. If you're ready to exit the Stress Spiral, let's go. It's time to start learning the strategies and rhythms that will help you thrive.

To do that, let's begin with focusing your time.

CHAPTER 2 IN A SNAP

- Even decently rested people who have friends and can bench-press a tiny house are stressed out.

- Time *off* won't heal you when the problem is how you spend your time *on*.

- Days off, vacations, and even sabbaticals aren't a complete solution for an unsustainable pace. A sustainable pace is the solution for an unsustainable pace.

- The Stress Spiral happens when you let yourself live with unfocused time, unleveraged energy, and hijacked priorities. It leaves you feeling overwhelmed, overcommitted, and overworked.

NO MORE CRAZY BUSY LIFE

- Unfocused time happens when you do your most important things randomly, squeezing them into leftover slots or sometimes not tackling them at all.

- The reason other people don't value your time is because you don't.

- Unleveraged energy springs from failing to cooperate with your personal energy levels as they rise and fall over the course of the day.

- Hijacked priorities happen when you allow other people to determine what you get done.

- The Thrive Cycle focuses your time, leverages your energy, and realizes your priorities so you can be at your best. It ensures you live in a way today that will help you thrive tomorrow.

- Focusing your time helps you get more accomplished in less time.

- Rather than competing with your energy levels, cooperate with them.

- When you leverage your energy, you'll realize you're capable of producing not just *more* work but much *better* work than you thought possible.

- Calendaring your energy zones, priorities, and key relationships will move everything you've learned from intention to reality.

- Winning at work while losing at home means you're losing. Period.

- You are at your most kind when you have the most margin.

- Living in the Thrive Cycle will free up between three hours a week and three hours a day of newly productive time. That could amount to more than a thousand additional productive hours each year.

PART 2

FOCUS YOUR TIME

YOU ACTUALLY DO HAVE THE TIME

Two Critical Mental Shifts About Time

I looked for balanced people doing anything good in
the world. I couldn't find many.

—Danielle Strickland

Let's take a short trip back to when I was stuck in the Stress
Spiral and felt like I never had the time to do what I needed to
get done—an era of my life when the principles of the Thrive
Cycle were still to be discovered. See whether any of this sounds
familiar . . .

I'm in my office. It's a scattered day, like the other days that
week.

I'm trying to write the forty-minute talk I have to deliver that
weekend. Being the pastor of a church is one of the few jobs in
the world that require writing a new forty-minute talk every
seven days. That's enough of a challenge in itself, but suddenly it's

hitting me that, for a message to really connect, it has to be compelling, profound, theologically deep, accessible to new people, original, faithful, and—if you want to engage people—funny and oh-so-charming too. So, you know . . . no pressure. Plus, I've been at this for over a decade. People know all my stories and all my jokes.

I'm not nearly finished. Meanwhile, the creative team is waiting on my input to finish planning the weekend services. All day there's been a line of people asking for five minutes of my time, which of course, is never five minutes. I'm preparing for a board meeting the next evening and a staff retreat the following week. And I've been playing Whack-a-Mole with my inbox. (Answer one email, and before I can hit Send, two more pop up.)

It's now past six in the evening. I've got the car keys in my hand, ready to head home because I'm already late for dinner, when my phone rings. I look at the phone screen. It's Rich, a member of my leadership team. I realize that if I don't take this call now, I'll have to put it on the ever-growing list of things I need to do tomorrow, which is supposed to be a day off.

I pick up the phone.

"Hey, Carey, I need your help on this project I'm working on."

I love Rich, but on this day, his request feels like the match that's going to light my internal powder keg. I put just enough empathy in my voice to not be completely rude but tell him, "As much as I'd love to, I just don't have the time. Sorry."

A civil response, I think, given the short fuse inside me. Little do I realize that will be one of the last times I ever say those words.

On my way home, I'm trying to not think about my highly ineffective day. Instead, my mind goes to a little book I've been reading about how the president of the United States spends his time. A friend told me it would be an interesting read, and although I think it was written for eighth graders, it's been a fun little book on everything from how meals are served in the White House to the daily briefing and how the Secret Service works.

As I get within a few blocks of home, a realization hits me hard enough to make me want to stop the car: *The president of the United States has exactly as many hours in a day as you do, Carey. No more, no less.*

That thought induces a deep panic in me.

How can you try to keep the economy afloat, hold a nation together, manage a nuclear arsenal, and work toward world peace (or at least stability) in just twenty-four hours a day?

Then this realization: *I'd be a disastrous president. Headline: "Nation Grinds to a Halt as President Suffers From Overwhelm, Unable to Finish Anything or Decide What to Eat for Breakfast."*

I chew on this for a while. A long while. That insight calls me out like few other insights ever have.

YOU'RE RICHER THAN YOU THINK

On any given day, I have precisely the same amount of time as any other person on planet Earth. And so, my friend, do you.

When it comes to time, you and I are rich. In fact, we're loaded. Time doesn't discriminate. With the two exceptions of the day you're born and the day you die, everyone gets exactly the same amount of time every day.

Think about the reverberations in your life:

- If the organization you're a part of grows to ten times its current size, you won't get a single extra hour to handle more stress.

- If you double the size of your family overnight, nobody is going to hand you an eighth day of the week to help you cope (although that would be super nice).
- If you become CEO of a *Fortune* 50 company, the universe will not give you a minute more to deal with the pressure.

The most productive people on Earth get the same amount of time you and I get. Which also means some people are *staggeringly* great at handling time. And me? Well, there was room for improvement. A lot of room.

Rather than wallowing in self-pity forever, I started rethinking what happened earlier that day.

I actually did have the time to help Rich. I just didn't take it.

I had the time to research my talk. And write it.

I definitely could have emptied my inbox and tackled a few other things on my to-do list.

I had all the time anyone else did.

Instead, I was so consumed by the requests coming at me, so distracted by the infinite sea of information that's available to anyone online, and so rattled by regular interruptions that I squandered the day. My time scattered in a million directions. I was so unfocused. I kept falling into the trap we all fall into: spending the most time on what matters least, and the least time on what matters most. I never intended to do that; it's just that's almost always what happens.

And my excuse? *I just don't have the time for that.* Well, that started to sound lamer and lamer. It simply wasn't true.

I had the time. I just didn't take it.

I was time rich. But I felt like I was broke.

MORE THAN JUST A TIME-MANAGEMENT STRATEGY

You might think that what follows is just time-management advice. It isn't. In some ways, prior to embracing the Thrive Cycle, I had already become a student of time management. I'd read books and articles, attended seminars, downloaded apps, and studied productivity. But the reality I kept bumping up against was the same problem you face: *the opportunities available to a capable person always exceed the time available.* Get around driven people, and you quickly realize many people also have more ambition than they have capacity. Maybe that describes you.

Traditional time management makes you more efficient, but it doesn't make you more effective over the long run. Efficiency fails because there's a fundamental limit, a wall you hit, in time management when all you're trying to do is to become more efficient. The limit is this: you're managing a *fixed* commodity. Which is why time management usually leaves you feeling drained, not energized. You're managing a growing list of demands with a limited asset.

Time doesn't grow. It won't expand, which is why time management brings you diminishing returns. People think money is a limited commodity. Well, yes. But not more limited than time. You can always make more money. You can never make more time.

To make matters more frustrating, once you become highly efficient, time *management* becomes demotivating because you have to settle for small—sometimes microscopic—improvements. Meanwhile, the opportunities you have or the responsibilities you carry continue to expand. *Then* what do you do?

In this chapter we'll explore two critical mental shifts. Changing how you focus time begins with changing how you think about time.

MENTAL SHIFT 1: TELL THE TRUTH ABOUT TIME

That day in the office was, for real, one of the last times I ever let myself say, "I don't have the time." Eliminating that statement (and others like it) forced me to tell the truth about time.

Listen to yourself and to the people around you to see how often you either say or hear statements like this:

"Sorry—I just don't have the time."

"I didn't have a chance to get it done."

"I wasn't able to finish it."

"I just can't."

"I wish I could. It's impossible."

Do you hear what those statements have in common?

Well, they're not entirely true. You could have. You just didn't.

Coming to terms with the truthfulness of how I thought and spoke about time was one of the hardest things I've had to do in my adult life. Getting dead honest about my time took away my excuses.

And I *loved* my excuses.

But you know what excuses do? They kill hopes, dreams, and goals.

Eliminate the excuses, and you start to move forward, because you can make excuses or you can make progress, but you can't make both.

So, start by telling yourself the truth. Pardon the drill sergeant for a moment, but take a few minutes and repeat after me:

I had the time. I didn't take it.

I had a chance to get it done. I didn't do it.

I was able to finish it. I just didn't.

I could. But I'm choosing not to.

It's not impossible. I'm just not making the time.

I'm *opting* to not meet.

I'm *deciding* to not work out.

I'm *choosing* to not go to the school play.

And there—you admitted it. To yourself.

I realize that's a pretty brutal level of honesty, but truth can be such a good friend. After all, of all the lies we tell, the lies we tell ourselves are most deadly. I don't know how to state how revolutionary telling the truth about time has been for me.

So, the first step to focusing your time is to start telling the truth about time. Stop saying you don't have the time. Start admitting you didn't make the time.

Stop saying you don't have the time. Start admitting you didn't make the time.

THE EMOTIONALLY INTELLIGENT TRUTH TELLER

So far this has been an interesting little mental exercise. But you and I need to make this work in everyday life. What does that look like? How might your newfound love of truth come out of your mouth in a way that doesn't alienate everyone you care about?

A quick word to the wise and socially adept. When you start admitting you didn't make the time to do something, it's probably best to reserve this truth for your *internal* dialogue. Telling people "I'm not going to make time for you" is an easy way to ruin your social life fast. Texting your best friend to let him know you've decided not to hang out with him on Friday is a really good way to lose a buddy. Instead, keep this kind of statement as a part of your dialogue with yourself when you're asked to give some of your time.

But notice the power in telling yourself the truth. When your mom invites you to lunch and you decide not to make time for her four weeks in a row, well, that tells you something. Lying to yourself about not having the time lets you off the hook. Telling yourself the truth will bump you into a rather sad reality: your mom isn't a priority. At least you know what you're dealing with then.

In a similar way, it's a good idea to adjust your explanations when you (inevitably) miss deadlines. I used to say things like "I didn't have a chance to get to it." These days, I say things like "I'm really sorry. I didn't make the time to complete the project. That's my bad. Let's talk about how I can turn that around." If you model this at work and at home, the attitudinal and verbal shifts involved in telling the truth about time can change the culture in a healthy way.

So here's the promise: it's okay to start dreaming again. At the end of this chapter, I'll challenge you to make a list of the things you've always wished you had more time for. When you start thinking about each request or opportunity with the understanding that you actually do have time for it, you'll sift through your priorities far more intentionally. Here are just a few examples:

- You have the time to work out.
- You have the time for a date night with your spouse.

to read
to d-report
in
hobbies

- You have the time to write a book.
- You have the time to plan a best-ever off-site with the team.
- You have the time to research and write that talk.
- You have the time to clean the garage.
- You have the time to pray and connect with God.
- You have the time to tuck your kids into bed at night after reading them a story.
- You have the time to thoughtfully change careers.

You have as much time as *anyone* else to do those things.

You have the time. The only question is whether you take it.

This truth changes even little things—things like your resentment level.

Before I made this shift, in a particularly busy season, I went for a ride on my road bike, pedaling hard while trying to squeeze in some exercise before my late-afternoon meeting. My mind was racing as I rode that sunny afternoon, trying to figure out how I was going to juggle everything on my plate.

As I rode through my neighborhood, I noticed two middle-aged guys sitting on a front porch, beverages in hand, chatting about whatever was on their minds . . . at two o'clock in the afternoon. They looked completely relaxed. Unlike me, they were totally enjoying the day.

You know what thought went through my head? *How on earth could two guys in the prime of their lives be sitting on a front porch on a beautiful day, enjoying themselves, when I'm so miserable while working so hard trying to get it all done?*

I used to throw a lot of pity parties. But here's what I realize now. I have the time to sit on my front porch too. I can relax any time I want, watching the world pass me by. And if I'm not doing that, it's because I chose not to do it and instead opted for something I felt was more valuable in that moment.

See the shift?

A second mental shift about time (and life) will help you adjust your mental map for the habits and strategies in the rest of the Thrive Cycle. Now that you're telling yourself the truth, it's time to shift your overall goal.

> ## MENTAL SHIFT 2: EMBRACE PASSION
> ## (AND ABANDON BALANCE)

There's a decent chance that at some point you decided to make living a balanced life your goal. Maybe you did it at New Year's or when you endured another grinding week and said "I've just got to find more balance" under your breath as you walked into the office to face whatever was ahead that day.

I'm going to suggest you do what I did: *abandon* balance as a goal. This is far more liberating than you might think.

Balance appears to be quite unreachable as a goal for most of us. Many people say they want it, but in an age when so much is coming at us at once and opportunity abounds and buzzing devices threaten to overtake even the quietest moments, most people never find the balance they dream of.

Much more significantly, though, balance in our culture appears to have morphed into a retreat rather than an advance. When you listen to what people who are seeking balance tend to say, they often speak of wanting *less:* less work, fewer commitments, or less effort. It's hard to build a meaningful life if you're constantly in retreat. I've noticed that when someone announces he or she has achieved a balanced life, I rarely find myself wanting to emulate that person.

who accomplish things

I have goals, and I don't want to retreat for the rest of my life. Do you? I want to accomplish something meaningful in my time here.

Conversely, think for a moment about people who accomplish significant things. Would you call them balanced people? For the most part, nope. *Passionate people*

Most people who accomplish significant things aren't *balanced* people; they're *passionate* people. Balanced people do "off" well, but being "off" isn't of much use if you have things you want to do that require you to be "on."

It's true that some passionate people have lives you may not want to fully emulate. Steve Jobs's monomaniacal passion may not be worth fully embracing, in the same way that Elon Musk's obsessive hours may not be a life goal. Both titans really struggled relationally. I run my desire to live a passionate life through my key spiritual, emotional, relational, physical, and even financial filters. Thriving is about more than making a dent in the universe while abandoning all the people around you to do so.

No, I want to choose my passions carefully and simply decide to embrace them fully. Which is why my wife and I schedule a weekly date night we almost never break. Which is why these days, when my kids are around, I want to give them my full focus. When we're throwing a dinner party, I want to be there, engaged with our friends and family. And when I'm writing a book, podcasting, speaking, or launching a venture, I want to pursue it fervently.

Whenever I decide to embrace something and allow it into my calendar and life, I'm inspired by these words, which some attribute to John Wesley: "Set yourself on fire with passion, and people will come from miles to watch you burn." My guess is you're fascinated by passionate people, whether famous passion-

54 FOCUS YOUR TIME

ate people or the coach you had in high school who breathed football or gymnastics and wouldn't quit until he or she saw your potential realized. As much as passionate entrepreneurs and leaders fascinate me, passion isn't just a work thing. Passion is what makes people hike a fourteener, decide to parent well, deepen their commitment to their spouse, coach Little League, or take on a social issue and fight for justice.

Balanced people don't change the world. Passionate people do.

So, what if you embraced everything you chose to do, not with resignation, indifference, or weariness but with passion? What would be different at work, at home, with your kids, with your faith, with your neighbors and best friends, if you dove into everything you chose to do with passion?

If you're going to take a break, take it. Enjoy it. If you're shooting for eight hours of rest, sleep deeply. Want to take a nap? Enjoy yourself. Don't feel guilty. Embrace it. Got a big project you're going to tackle at work? Throw your heart into it.

Balanced people don't change the world. Passionate people do.

The key to living passionately is to focus your time on what is truly most important to you and to choose to do those things wholeheartedly, with enthusiasm. Stress makes you skim. Weariness wears you out, and when you have nothing left to give, it's too easy to coast.

Embracing passion also means you'll have to limit the things you decide to do. Thriving calls for a wholehearted embrace not of more but of *less,* done well. Of a few highly focused priorities you are passionate about. As Greg McKeown said, "I can do anything but not everything."[1]

Which means the best strategy is to focus your time on the things and people that matter most. When you allow something into your calendar and life, make it a new goal to pursue it *passionately.*

YOU NEVER HAVE ENOUGH TIME FOR ... WHAT?

Now that you know you have the time for what matters most (because you realize your time bank account is loaded), we're going to get hyperpractical. I want you to write down what matters most to you in the Dream List chart on the following page.

Use the chart to list the most important things and people that are getting squeezed out of your life. In the left column, write down a list of three to five tasks, projects, or people you wish you had more time for. In the right column, write down approximately how much time each week you'd like to devote to each goal, in hours per week. Doing that is going to be key, because then the rest of the book won't seem like an academic theory. You'll have an end in mind, some ways your life will actually be different and better. And more immediately, in the next chapter, you'll learn how to identify your most valuable hours in the day so you can accomplish what you're about to write down. Pinpointing those hours will help you get started right away.

So, start writing. Dream a little. What and who will become a new or renewed part of your life as you move forward? After all, you've got as much time as anyone else does to passionately pursue what matters. And if you free up between three hours a week and three hours a day in newly productive hours, you'll be able to turn some of your desires into reality.

MY DREAM LIST

PRIORITY	TIME
Person/task I wish I had more time for	Approximate hours per week needed
Read JW	
Long mp 1 x/wk	

CHAPTER 3 IN A SNAP

- When it comes to time, you and I are rich. In fact, we're loaded. Time doesn't discriminate. With the two exceptions of the day you're born and the day you die, everyone gets exactly the same amount of time every day.

- The opportunities available to a capable person always exceed the time available.

- Time doesn't grow. It won't expand, which is why time management brings you diminishing returns.

- You can make excuses or you can make progress, but you can't make both.

- Stop saying you don't have the time. Start admitting you didn't make it.

- Most people who accomplish significant things aren't *balanced* people; they're *passionate* people.

- Balanced people don't change the world. Passionate people do.

CHAPTER 4

FIND YOUR GREEN ZONE

How to Uncover When You're at Your Best

Someone once asked Somerset Maugham if he wrote on a schedule or only when struck by inspiration. "I write only when inspiration strikes," he replied. "Fortunately it strikes every morning at nine o'clock sharp."

That's a pro.

—Steven Pressfield

I have this problem, or as my sometimes sleep-challenged wife might say, this gift. I can fall asleep almost anywhere, anytime. Including highly inappropriate times.

Just ask my staff. A few years ago, I was interviewing a prospective hire. According to my operations manager, who was with me for the interview, I dozed off *while I was conducting the interview.* She's never let me live it down.

In my defense, I was at a Chili's in Scranton and it was almost midnight. (I know—this sounds like an episode of *The Office.* Don't ask.) I'd also spoken at an event earlier that evening after a seven-hour drive to get to Pennsylvania, so there's that. And not to throw shade on my colleague, but I might question her ability to accurately assess someone else's state of wakefulness after 11:00 p.m. Still, point taken. You probably shouldn't fall asleep while conducting job interviews.

I couldn't focus. I could barely stay awake. The problem? The time of day—or lack of day in my case. I'm far from my best at night. Swing by a dinner party at my place for further evidence. My conversation will be less than scintillating after nine o'clock.

Which leads us to a helpful truth. Your energy waxes and wanes over your waking hours. Time feels different at different stages during the day.

At some point in your life, you probably slotted yourself into one of the two great categories of human beings who walk this planet: early bird or night owl. Some people are comatose in the morning. Others, like me, struggle to stay awake after the sun sets.

Daniel Pink has done a fantastic study of how people perform at different times of the day in his book *When: The Scientific Secrets of Perfect Timing.* According to Pink, about 14 percent of people are morning people, 21 percent are night owls, and 65 percent of us are somewhere in the middle.[1] While knowing whether you're a morning person or night owl can help, what if leveraging your time could result in far more productivity?

NOT ALWAYS AT YOUR BEST

Even though you have twenty-four equal hours in the day, not all hours *feel* equal. You're wide awake for the 10:00 a.m. meeting, but at 2:30 that afternoon, you've got toothpicks wedged in your eyelids to stay alert for the conference call and you're jiggling your leg to remind yourself to stay focused. You sprint through some hours and drag yourself through others.

If you double-click on that reality, it becomes even more alarming.

As I got better at focusing my time post-burnout and monitoring how I was *really* doing, I noticed I have only three to five hours a day when I'm truly at my best—alert, alive, focused, flowing with good ideas, and feeling like I'm at my peak. No matter how hard I tried or how rested I was, I was deeply productive for only a three- to five-hour window.

At first, that observation made me feel like a fraud. If I get paid for full-time work and put in eight or more hours a day, how can I have only three to five peak hours in a day? Then I started diving deeper. After doing more research and testing this theory with other leaders I've trained, guess what? Most people have only three to five deeply productive hours in a day when their energy is at its peak. That's it.

Claire Diaz-Ortiz, who worked at Twitter in the start-up years, made a similar observation: even the most brilliant Silicon Valley engineers have about three creative and highly productive hours in them daily.[2] Cal Newport, author of *Deep Work,* has researched this quite extensively and argued that our capacity for intense, focused work comes in at around four hours a day.[3]

Most people have only three to five deeply productive hours in a day when their energy is at its peak. That's it.

So, this appears to be a universal phenomenon, affecting even—gasp—doctors, nurses, and surgeons. Friend to friend, if you ever have to go for surgery, ask for the 9:00 a.m. appointment, not the 3:00 p.m. slot. Anesthesiologists (the doctors who put you under for surgery) have an "adverse event" about 1 percent of the time at 9:00 a.m. At 4:00 p.m., the rate rises to 4.2 percent. You're over four times more likely to have a problem in the afternoon procedure than if they work on you in the morning. The culprit? Researchers point to the physicians' circadian rhythms that make focusing harder in the afternoon.

Similarly, studies of colonoscopy accuracy (colonoscopies were once artfully described to me by a friend as the art of having a garden hose stuck up your butt) show that endoscopists detect polyps (the growths that can indicate cancer) at a lower rate as the day progresses. Every hour produces a 5 percent reduction in detection.[4]

The reality of having three to five peak productive hours each day really resonates with the leaders I've trained over the last few years as well. Outside of one person who told me she thought she had six highly productive hours a day (I'm a little envious), the rest of us appear to confirm the three-to-five-hour observation.

What do you do with this rather sobering reality?

FIND YOUR GREEN ZONE

As we saw in chapter 2, you can cooperate with natural timing or compete with it. It's going to be way more fun (and less deadly, if you're a doctor) if you cooperate with it. The first step is to uncover when that three-to-five-hour window when you're at your best happens for you. That's your Green Zone—something you'll come to value, protect, and leverage.

As I started to pay more attention to when I did my best work, it didn't take long to recognize that I am normally pretty sharp between 7:00 and 11:00 a.m. I noticed my stamina typically dips in the late morning, before lunch. To offset the dip in energy and focus, I often take a short nap after lunch. For me, taking a nap is like plugging my phone back in. I may not get back to 100 percent, but even fifteen minutes can refuel me to 85 percent for a while.

After a nap, I'm usually better for an hour or two, but as the afternoon wears on, my energy level typically drops again, and by 4:00 p.m. it's hard to focus on any important tasks (let alone do surgery . . . I'm joking). After dinner, my energy surges a little again, but once nine rolls around most days, I'm pretty much done. Movie nights cost me extra money as I doze through the film and end up having to watch it twice.

Your day will follow patterns too. Those patterns will be different from mine, but the point is that they're probably quite consistent. They repeat almost daily.

Eventually I noticed my patterns were so predictable that I could put them on a clock. So I did (and so can you). Let's call it the Energy Clock—a clock that details when your energy peaks and dips. The hours and patterns will vary, but the principle prevails: your day has peak energy periods, mid-energy hours, and some bleak moments. Mapping it on a clock makes it easy to see what a typical day looks like (and feels like) for you.

Have a look at the Energy Clock below. It outlines my unique patterns. Again, yours will vary. The key is to figure out and plot when you are at your best. On the twelve-hour clock below, the Green Zones represent high energy, the Yellow Zones reflect midlevel energy, and the Red Zone plots low energy. Note: The Energy Clock represents your daytime pattern, so see the day outlined on the clock as beginning at 6:00 a.m. (the top of the clock) and ending at 5:59 p.m. That way, it maps your energy as it ebbs and flows through the typical waking day. If you want, you can copy the clock to develop a version for the other twelve hours as well. (Night owls or insomniacs may want to do that. My 6:00 p.m. to 6:00 a.m. clock would be a sea of yellow and mostly red.)

For example, here's what my daytime clock looks like:

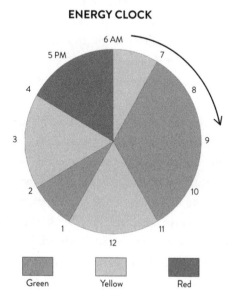

ENERGY CLOCK

And now the main point: Any idea when your best three to five hours in the day are? When you're at your worst? When you're in the middle? There's no *right* answer here. The important thing is to find *your* answer. Your Energy Clock will help you find more of a breakthrough than you think. Later in this chapter, you'll be able to download your own personal Energy Clock, but first, I'll explain a little more context and information about it.

Tracking both your *productivity* and your *mood* is the key to figuring out your personal zones. While we all have good days and bad days, your Green Zone hours are generally characterized by a combination of high productivity and good spirits—a flow that marks both your output and your state of mind.

Observing how you repeatedly behave will lead you to categorize the hours that make it into your Energy Clock. Naturally, there will be variations each day, depending on how much sleep you got the night before, how much stress you're feeling, whether it's a "normal" week or you have some unusual things planned. Similarly, you'll have weeks when a personal or work crisis gets you spiraling or a thunderstorm wakes you up at 4:00 a.m. But overall, you'll see that your energy rises and falls in predictable patterns. So does your mood.

You can evaluate your productivity by looking at . . .

- The quality and flow of your ideas when brainstorming, writing, crafting, or creating anything—from a talk to an agenda to a proposal or plan.
- Your focus. Are you highly focused? Distracted? Moderately zoned in?
- Your ability to generate helpful or even breakthrough ideas that move your mission forward.
- How well you lead or contribute to meetings.

- How long it takes you to clear an inbox and write thoughtful, intelligent responses.
- How insightful and helpful you are in your interactions with other people.
- How quickly you move things off your task list.

When it comes to tracking your mood, you'll also notice ebbs and flows over the course of the day. With some personalities, the variation will be slight: you're normally cheery or normally grumpy, but in some windows you're a little less cheery or a little more grumpy. With other personality types, the mood fluctuations might be greater.

As you track your mood throughout the day and evening, pay attention to . . .

- How you interact with your colleagues at work.
- How you engage your family at home.
- How you feel about your job . . . even your favorite part of your job.
- Your spirits: Are you in good spirits, poor spirits, or somewhere in the middle?
- Your self-talk (your thoughts about yourself).
- The way you interact with strangers (on the street, in public places, or how you behave in your car in traffic).

I've found it helpful to not just pay attention to my own impressions but also get input from others. Often other people (your coworkers, your boss, your family) see things about you that you'll miss (like your mood, for example, or how you perform in meetings). So be sure to ask them.

To help you identify each zone in your life, here are some

working definitions of the three zones and what you're looking to find in each.

Green Zone: High Energy

The Green Zone is when your energy is high, your mind is clear, your focus is sharp, and you find it easy to think and to imagine, to contribute and to create. Your mindset is fresh and positive. You have the physical energy for work and for life: you feel like going for a run or ride, getting on top of the burning project at work, holding that critical meeting, making your plan for the next quarter, writing that next chapter of your book, or having that strategic one-on-one. When you're in your high-energy zone, you have enthusiasm for the tasks ahead. But even more than that, you're focused and strong enough to tackle them well. To put it simply, your Green Zone is those handful of hours a day when you're at your best.

When many or most of the following characteristics are present, you're in your Green Zone.

Green Zone productivity characteristics:

- creative
- alert
- engaged
- efficient
- effective
- productive
- accurate

Green Zone mood characteristics:

- kind
- optimistic

- cheerful
- thoughtful
- helpful
- generous

The hours when you're at your most productive and in your most positive frame of mind are your Green Zone. Remember, you're looking for only three to five hours. Don't try to pretend you're superhuman and have eight.

If it makes you feel better, I never have more than five. If you overstretch your zones, the rest of what you'll learn in this book will work against you, not for you. I promise you that three leveraged hours will beat ten unleveraged hours. So, as hard as it is, be realistic about your limits. You'll thank yourself later.

Red Zone: Low Energy

Contrast how you feel in your Green Zone with a window when your energy is low. When you have low energy, you struggle to pay attention: you zone out easily, you have a hard time following what's going on, and you might not even be listening in meetings. Not only do you struggle to produce your best work, but sometimes when your energy is low, you struggle to produce *any* meaningful work—even emptying your email inbox feels impossible. In a low-energy window, you have to force yourself to work out, make yourself cut the grass, or talk yourself into prepping dinner. Bottom line: you just don't have the energy for it.

Red Zone productivity characteristics:

- not creative
- tired
- disengaged
- inefficient

- ineffective
- unproductive
- low accuracy

Red Zone mood characteristics:

- frustrated
- pessimistic
- short-tempered
- selfish
- unwilling
- stingy

Recognize your Red Zone? Sadly, we all have one. I promise you, if you don't recognize your Red Zone, your colleagues and family probably do. Just ask them when you're usually irritable and unhelpful. They know.

Yellow Zone: Mid Energy

The middle ground is what we'll call the Yellow Zone. When you're in the Yellow Zone, you're neither at your best nor at your worst. You're—no surprise here—in the middle. You're fine in meetings. You can produce content or plan ahead, even if it's not your best effort. You can plug away at chores both at work and at home, but you feel neither deeply focused and alert nor terrible. Your work tends to be in the middle too—good but not remarkable.

Yellow Zone productivity characteristics:

- moderately creative
- awake
- partially engaged

- fairly efficient
- relatively effective
- mostly productive
- somewhat accurate
- producing decent work

Yellow Zone mood characteristics:

- pleasant
- realistic
- civil
- introspective
- slightly bothered by others
- somewhat generous

Your Yellow Zone is not a wasteland. It's a place where a lot of good things can and will get done. Just not your best things. It's also often more than half your waking life, so understanding when you're in it can have an immense payoff.

WHEN ARE YOU AT YOUR BEST?

So, now that you've noted the characteristics of each zone, take some time over the next few days (or even weeks) to finesse your personal Energy Clock. Plotting out your personal Energy Clock is important because it's the key to helping you discover *when* you're at your best. In my experience, some people intuitively know what their zones are (you may already have them mapped out in your head). Others have a vague idea. But some people have never thought about it, and it takes them awhile to figure it out.

While this isn't a universal rule, I've found that the younger you are, the more time it takes to figure out the specific windows. That's not surprising for a couple of reasons. First, when you're in your twenties, you have a pretty strong overall energy level. Second, self-awareness often grows as you age, so if you're young, this may be the first time you've even considered the issue or paid attention to what your mind and body are telling you about your energy. Don't worry if you've never turned your mind to this. Regardless of your age, you're about to give yourself a serious advantage by going through this exercise.

Now's the time to figure out your personal zones and plot them out on your personal Energy Clock.

▼ Download your free, customizable Energy Clock at
www.AtYourBestToday.com

A few notes. Don't get too bogged down in details. You don't need to worry about going from Green to Yellow at 10:47 a.m. every day and then perhaps dipping into the Red Zone from 11:18 to 11:29 a.m. Broad blocks of hours are fine. Also, don't worry about being 100 percent accurate. Like everything you'll learn in the Thrive Cycle, your Energy Clock can be adjusted. Or perhaps you get a new mattress that gives you better sleep and changes how you feel or a promotion that shifts everything. Awesome. Again, you can adjust your Energy Clock as you or the things around you change.

You're going to come back to your Green Zone again and again in this book. If you don't really know what it is, you won't leverage the ideas in this book as much as you could. As a friend once told me, the value of a book like this is like the value of paint: it's all in the application. In the same way a basement full of unopened gallons of paint does nothing to transform your home, unapplied strategies do nothing to change your life. So, spend some time now plotting out your Energy Clock. You'll be glad you did.

HOW TO WASTE YOUR GREEN ZONE

Before we move into how to use your Green Zone in the next chapter, let me show you how *not* to use it. Before I realized I had a Green Zone or figured out what to do with it, I did what most people do with their best energy and hours: I spent them unthinkingly and randomly.

Before I developed the Green Zone concept, on some days I'd use my best hours exercising. On other days I'd write. Still other days I'd do meetings or run early-morning errands (do you know how few lines there are in stores at 7:00 a.m.?).

I was also the king of breakfast meetings. After all, I was going to eat, so why not make that time productive?

While I sincerely loved my breakfast meetings, my most important work—writing talks and strategic planning—waited until I got back to the office.

Plus, you know how breakfast meetings go. They look innocent on the calendar, but audit how much time and energy they really take, and this is what it looks like:

6:30—Drive to the restaurant

7:00—Meeting

8:00—Meeting goes a little longer than you expected because you're having fun

8:30—Leave the restaurant

8:45—Grab coffee at a drive-through

9:00—Get to the office and immediately get bombarded by what you missed and the staff who have shown up

10:00—Turn your mind to your most important work
11:03—Already tired and want to go home

The same pattern happened if I drove to the gym or went for an hour-long bike ride or ran errands. By the time I got ready, did the activity, got back, showered, and focused, hours had ticked by. My most productive window of the day was gone, and my most important work remained untouched.

I've also worked with some otherwise very smart people who use their Green Zone to push through a list of the things they hate most. They'll take their prime hours to address a clogged inbox, submit their expense report, or organize their files. That's great if your job is to answer email, file expenses, or organize hard drives—but most of these leaders are doing those jobs only to get them out of the way. And they waste some of their best hours doing so.

Sound familiar? You already know that if you want to be at your best, things are going to have to change.

THE THREE-HOUR WORKDAY

If you don't want to waste your precious Green Zone, what do you do when all you really have is three to five peak hours a day? Embrace a three-hour workday? Resign? Admit to your boss that you're a fake?

Moving to a three-hour workday might sound awesome, but most of us get paid to show up for a little longer than that. You still have another twentyish hours left on the clock—hours you need to spend on other things.

Which raises some great questions. What *do* you do in your Red Zone when you're slumping at your desk after a heavy-carb lunch or dozing off at your third grader's school play—other than caffeinate? What about your Yellow Zone, when you're not quite as sharp as in your Green Zone but not exactly one of the walking dead yet? What about your inbox? All those calls you have to make? That oil change that was due last Tuesday? Your family? Hobbies?

What you do is leverage your energy (or lack of it). Don't fight the patterns; *fuel* them. Use each zone to its maximum advantage, and yes, despite its apparent lack of promise, even your Red Zone can be used strategically. We'll explore all that and more in the next couple of chapters.

CHAPTER 4 IN A SNAP

- Even though you have twenty-four equal hours in a day, not all hours *feel* equal.

- Most people have three to five deeply productive hours in a day.

- Green Zone: When your energy is high. Your mind is clear, and your focus is sharp.

- Three leveraged hours beats ten unleveraged hours.

- Red Zone: When your energy is low. You struggle to pay attention, and you find it very difficult to produce meaningful work.

- Yellow Zone: When your energy is in the middle. You're neither at your best nor at your worst.

- The value of this book's principles is like the value of paint: it's all in the application.

- Leverage your energy (or lack of it). Don't fight the patterns; *fuel* them.

PART 3

LEVERAGE YOUR ENERGY

DO WHAT YOU'RE BEST AT

Investing Your Energy for the Highest Returns

> You must match time's swiftness with your speed in using it, and you must drink quickly as though from a rapid stream that will not always flow.
>
> —Seneca

Making the right investments with your time and energy can produce some astounding returns, like making the right financial investments does. On that point, let's play a game. Imagine you have ten different stocks in your retirement fund. Let's also imagine that two of the ten stocks happen to be producing 80 percent of the return you've been getting. Wanting to be sure you're seeing things right, you go back through your records and see that for five years these stocks have consistently produced 80 percent of the growth of your investments. You then meet with your investment adviser, and she affirms how these stocks are solid investments moving forward. You google some other reports showing that these two stocks are likely to continue growing. Now you're convinced. This is not an aberration.

You have $1,000 to invest today. What would you do?

One option is to ignore the data you've just seen, put $100 into each of the ten stocks, and plan on retiring at age ninety-two.

Personally, I would put 100 percent of my money into the two stocks that are producing most of the results (disclosure: I'm no Warren Buffett, but I'm a bit of a risk-taker). If you're a little more cautious, you might put 80 percent of the money into the high-performing investments and distribute the remaining $200 elsewhere.

To sum it up, given what you know, putting $100 into each of the ten stocks just doesn't make sense, does it?

Here's the point: while most people wouldn't invest their money unthinkingly, so many people do invest their time and energy unthinkingly.

Investing your highest-yield activities in your Green Zone can produce returns similar to those two stocks. While you have twenty-four equal hours in a day, not all hours *feel* equal or *produce* equally. Leveraging your energy is where the exponential returns begin. Doing your best work while you have your best energy significantly boosts the quality of your work, the quantity of your work (you'll likely be able to tackle more), and even your mood.

By now, I trust you've sketched out the first version of your Energy Clock and have a sense of what your Green Zone is—those three to five hours when you find yourself at your peak energy most days. You also have a decent sense of your Yellow (mid energy) and Red (low energy) Zones. We'll come back to your Yellow and Red Zones in the next chapter, but now we're going to drill down on the best use of your Green Zone, because that's where most of the power is.

While you have twenty-four equal hours in a day, not all hours feel equal or produce equally.

YOU'RE BEST AT ... WHAT?

Now that you know *when* you're at your best, let's crack the code on the other important factor: *What* exactly are you best at?

I realize that sounds like a simple question, but not everyone can answer it accurately. It's probably true that the older you are, the more aware you are of your strengths and weaknesses. But I've also discovered after twenty-five years in senior leadership that I am still refining my understanding of what I'm best at. Every time I do that (and get it right), the yield increases. Discovering what you're best at may well be a lifetime pursuit. I have a mentor who is in his eighties, and his exceptionally clear understanding of his gifting has him making meaningful contributions to leaders around the world in his ninth decade. I'd call that a worthy goal. In addition, personal growth and career transitions both require people to keep honing their understanding of what they're best at.

To be sure, there's something inside all of us that wants to be great at everything, and while I've met a few polymaths, that's not me. Put me on the spot, and with little prep, I can deliver a stirring vision talk that can motivate people to action. But ask me to fix the brakes on your car, and let's hope your insurance is paid up. Most of us have a narrow range of things we excel at.

While your gifting is probably narrower than you hoped it would be (don't worry—a narrow gifting can be a superpower), there are other factors to consider when figuring out what the best use of your Green Zone is—factors like passion and impact.

Gifting + Passion + Impact = Optimal Green Zone Focus.

If you Venn diagram it, it comes together like this:

OPTIMAL GREEN ZONE

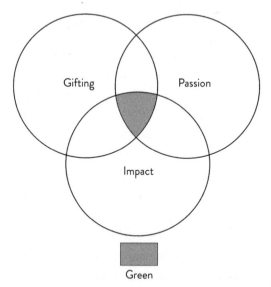

Let's break that down one component at a time, beginning with your gifting.

GIFTING

Your *gifting* is your sweet spot—what you uniquely do best.[1] Those are the things that others find difficult but you make look easy, the things for which you have natural aptitude.

Your gifting is different from your skill set. Skills are both things you can learn (such as woodworking or project management), or deeper developments of your natural gifting (such as a talented singer who takes voice lessons or a new CEO who hires a performance coach). Skill development can get you far. We'll come back to how to use your skill set at the end of this chapter. For now, though, focus on gifting. Gifting is a much more natural or raw level of talent than a skill set is.

Here's how gifting works (and doesn't work). I had always wanted to play guitar when I was a kid, and I even brought a twelve-string with me to college. With three years of hard work on chord progressions, I learned to play the first two minutes of Journey's "Don't Stop Believin'." Most of my friends couldn't recognize it (largely because it was a keyboard piece with some electric guitar thrown in), but hey, I gave it my all. Eventually I put my guitar away and forgot about it.

That is, until I was thirty-six. That's the year my wife and I decided to get our son Jordan, who was ten, an electric guitar for Christmas. Deciding to spare no expense, we went to Costco and got the best Yamaha they had. It was a start.

Jordan had been in music lessons since he was a kindergartner and has natural musical talent. As his dad, I thought this would be my chance to show him both chords I remembered from college and to learn guitar with him. We were, after all, starting out from almost the same place—he'd never played guitar, and I barely knew how in the first place. I thought we could learn in tandem.

I looked at the chord charts we bought with the guitar and amp and put together a C and G, slowly and clumsily moving up and down the fretboard. He asked for the guitar and, after one or two fumbles, found the C and G. He then discovered D and E and was soon progressing into minors and sharps, at which point I retreated to the corner to sob. My brilliant idea of father and son learning together and becoming guitar heroes together lasted eight minutes.

Jordan is musically gifted. I'm, well, not. No amount of skill can really make up for a lack of natural talent. My son went on to play not only keys and guitar but drums and bass too. He even recorded with a few bands. Me? I continue to listen to Journey.

One clue to your gifting is that something that seems effortless to you is difficult or complex for others. To this day, when I see an artist playing an instrument and singing at the same time, I'm in awe. When I see a golfer hit a 320-yard drive straight down the middle, I applaud (applaud from the woods, that is, where I'm still looking for my ball). One of my longtime staff members, Sarah, can defuse almost any situation with her grace, warmth, and empathy, so whenever the stakes are high, I call on her.

All that stuff looks hard, if not impossible, to me. Yet when I deliver a forty-five-minute keynote at a conference in front of thousands of people and don't use notes, people ask, "How do you do that?" I often want to say, "It's not that hard. It just comes to me."

To find your gifting, ask yourself and people close to you these questions:

- *What seems effortless to me that seems difficult or complex to others?*
- *What talent do I keep using in different settings?* (For ex-

ample, you end up organizing events, speaking to or for the group, or being the manager even if you weren't hired to do that.)

- *What do other people affirm in me as my gifting and talent?*

PASSION

Your *passion* is what you love to do. But what about tasks—the actual work you have to do? Well, in the same way that not all hours are created equal, not all tasks are created equal. You love some things you do, and you loathe some things you do. That's normal.

You're probably passionate about the things you're gifted at, but passion can extend beyond gifting. The key to finding your passion is to look for things that give you energy. In other words, there are a handful of things you do that you find not only enjoyable but also energizing. While they might be challenging tasks (like crafting a fantastic profit-and-loss statement, closing a deal, or climbing a mountain), you find doing them invigorating.

Your passion can be almost anything. While communication is my key passion, yours might be strategic planning, team development, organization, event planning, editing, administration, design, teaching, or something else entirely. In your personal life, it might be running, cooking, art, or time with friends or family. You feel like you simply have to do it.

If you're not sure what your passion is, monitor your thought life and the things you say to others for clues about your passion. Maybe you say things like, "Oh good, today I get to meet with Jake. I love building into him," or, "So glad I get three hours to design my client's new web page today." There are clues in thoughts like that, clues about your passion. It could be that you like Jake or like building into people or both. Similarly, you might like working with clients or web design or both. Pay attention to the things that fuel you.

I recently wrapped up a day of filming where I shot ten new talks for various online events. Sure, it was a tiring day. But as the crew and I wrapped up, I felt like I had done what I was created to do: deliver leadership content in a way that could help people. To quote Olympic gold medalist runner Eric Liddell in the classic *Chariots of Fire* movie, "I believe that God made me for a purpose. . . . He also made me fast. And when I run, I feel His pleasure."[2]

Hard as it may be, passion means you can't imagine not doing it, and despite the effort, you find it immensely rewarding. When I hit Publish on a new podcast episode, help my team go further, or release a new book, I still have a hard time believing I get to do this with my life.

In my personal life, time with my wife, kids, family, and friends as well as activities like boating, barbecuing, and cycling always make my list of things I'm passionate about. I hope you've got a list of things you love to do in your personal time.

To identify your passion, ask yourself these questions:

- *What tasks do I most look forward to doing?*
- *What things energize me as I do them?*
- *When do I lose track of time because I'm enjoying what I'm doing so much?*

IMPACT

Finally, the best way to use your Green Zone is to leverage it for the biggest impact. *Impact* refers to those things that, when done, will make the biggest difference, sometimes in the moment but often long term.

highest value tasks

So how do you determine impact? Ask yourself what the (highest-value tasks are) that your employer pays you to accomplish. What are your core responsibilities? What are your overriding goals? Those are great refocusing questions. Once you get a sense of how to answer them, you probably realize what many leaders have discovered: these are the easiest things to sacrifice in the rush of a busy day. The most important tasks you're charged with are the very things you don't always get done.

At work, maybe you desperately need the next quarter to be a growth quarter, or you realize that aligning your team around the mission and objectives would really move your organization forward. Perhaps you sense that your most important clients need better nurturing, that it's time to craft a vision talk, or that you've simply got to get the rebranding done or the new office opened or the strategic plan completed. Instinctively you sense that there are a few things that, when done, will move the needle more than other things. So, the question becomes, How can you leverage your gifting and passion to make progress on these most important things during your Green Zone hours?

When it comes to determining what has the greatest impact personally, you can begin with this question: What am I trying to accomplish with my life, my family, my faith? I realize this is a huge question, but it's important to keep in focus. Then figure out what you need to do to move closer to your goals in the moment.

Practically, as a parent, you might realize that quality time with your kids is what they need right now. Or maybe it's the opposite. Because you've had *sooooo* much time with the kids, you need time away with a healthy dose of adult conversation or a morning all to yourself so you don't turn on your kids. If you're a person of faith, maybe elevating the spiritual disciplines that have been falling through the cracks would be a great use of your Green Zone. When you devote your Green Zone to these important personal goals, you'll see far better results than if you pursue them in your non-optimal time. You'll feel only half as refreshed if you do your most important activities in your Yellow or Red Zone. Using your Green Zone for key objectives brings powerful results.

Getting a sense of what might have the biggest impact for you at work and at home? Awesome.

To find what's most important, ask yourself these questions:

- *What can I do today/in this season that will have a significantly positive impact?*[3]
- *What few things (or one thing), when done well, will help me move the cause forward?*
- *What activities, when I repeatedly do them, help me make meaningful progress? (This is a key question because your ongoing patterns and disciplines often make the biggest impact on your work and life.)*

So . . . there it is. Gifting + Passion + Impact = Optimal Green Zone Focus.

If you want a more formal way to assess what you're best at, use the "Optimal Green Zone Focus" cheat sheet.

▼ Download your "Optimal Green Zone Focus" cheat sheet at
www.AtYourBestToday.com

As you answer the questions related to these three areas and use your Green Zone accordingly, you'll leverage the power of doing what you're best at when you're at your best.

A quick note not to be too hard on yourself in tackling these questions. For all you perfectionist types, you don't need to have flawless answers. Do the best you can; then revisit this section of the book. The Thrive Cycle and Green Zone improve as you learn more about yourself and as you revisit the key concepts and principles, adjusting as you go.

LEVERAGE IT

Here's how an optimal Green Zone comes together. Let's say you're a software engineer who is working on an app that goes to market in two months. You're charged with overseeing the user interface (UI). As you move into the home stretch, you realize the best use of your Green Zone is to do three things: You need to do some final market research on how the UI is expected to evolve in the next twelve to eighteen months so your app doesn't feel outdated quickly; you set aside sixty minutes a day for that. Next, you spend sixty to ninety minutes poring over the feedback from beta users to make sure you catch glitches and understand what their experience, good and bad, has been. Because you're using your Green Zone, you're fully engaged with the feedback, and you take detailed notes. Finally, you set aside the rest of your Green Zone for two meetings: an hour with your project lead and thirty minutes with the entire team to gather their feedback, overcome obstacles, and set the next objectives.

When you think about it, that's a pretty fair day's work. And sure, you have other meetings and activities that you'll tackle in your Yellow and Red Zones, but if that's all you got accomplished for the day, that's a pretty good day. You'll be shocked at how often that happens when you optimize your Green Zone.

Now to flip to your personal life for a moment, let's imagine a Saturday when you have yard work, kids' homework, and a much-needed connection with your spouse before everyone heads to an afternoon football game. Again, let's imagine that your Green Zone happens in the morning and that your spouse values quality time. Having breakfast with her at a favorite coffee shop gives you two hours of uninterrupted time—her love language. When you get home, you spend half an hour with the kids on their homework and then cut the grass (when you're not at your best, but hey, you're not in a competitive lawn-cutting league). You grab a quick nap and then head off to the football game.

Most people let days happen to them, which results in disappointment, tension, unmet expectations, and important things left undone. By leveraging your Green Zone, you can make sure that doesn't happen to you.

ROOKIES VERSUS GREEN ZONE PROS

We left the issue of skill behind a few pages ago. Let's pick it up again, because this is where it really gets fun. If you want to see your Green Zone used to its maximum potential, don't just think about what gifts you can use in your Green Zone, but think about the ones you can develop.

Malcolm Gladwell explained how world-class performers develop their gifts in *Outliers,* the book in which he popularized what's become widely known as "the ten-thousand-hour rule." Gladwell argued that becoming world class at something—truly mastering a craft—is a combination of raw gifting and putting in ten thousand hours working on that craft.[4]

Which means that, if you're going to really develop your gift, you practice when everyone else is off playing. It means working on communication, not just to get your next talk done but to study the craft of speaking and writing more deeply. It means rehearsing the talk to an empty room. Wordsmithing your work until it sings and soars. Working through eight drafts, not just two. If you're a pro golfer, it means chipping and putting until the sun sets and all the other golfers have gone home. If you're serious about your relationships, it means going to a counselor to work on things rather than just watching Netflix after complaining to your friend about how bad your relationship is. Gifted people who put in ten thousand hours of practice and development are far more likely to become top of their field. That, Gladwell argued, is one of the consistent stories behind success.

There's only one problem I have with developing my gift (and my Green Zone). Naturally, I do the *opposite* of what Gladwell argued you should do to become world class at something.

Back to my life as a communicator.

My father likes to tell the story of me at age twelve being asked to give a talk to our church one night about my experience at camp. (I have no real recollection of it, so you'll have to trust my dad's account.) Apparently, that night, I was far down on the list of speakers, and as the girl ahead of me finished up, I leaned over and told my dad that she had just said everything I was going to say.

My dad looked concerned and replied, "Well, Carey, what are you going to do?"

Foreshadowing too much of the rest of my life, twelve-year-old me apparently said, "Don't worry, Dad. I'll make something up." Which I then proceeded to do. My dad and everyone else in the church hall that night thought I had prepared a great speech.

While that sounds like a great ability, it has a dark side. Here's my problem: *I can still do that.* If you pulled me aside this afternoon and said, "Carey, the speaker for the final session at the event just called in sick. Can you fill in? We need a thirty-minute keynote about five minutes from now. You up for it?"

Sure, I'd swallow hard, and I don't want to sound arrogant, but I think I could do it. And most people would probably walk away satisfied and say it was helpful.

Which is exactly the problem. The more naturally gifted you are at something, the easier it is to spend *less* time on it, not more. Why? Because you can do a good job without even trying.

Far too often in my life, I've done just that. I whipped something together because I got overwhelmed with so many other things and I had so many other priorities vying for my attention. I threw a talk together in a quarter of the time I should have taken to do it well. And often nobody noticed. That's a terrible way to steward a gift. It's also a really bad long-term strategy if you want to fully develop your talent.

The tyranny of the everyday usually gets in the way of developing your gift into a high-level skill set. Physicians who spend all day seeing patients can end up doing the bare minimum of continuing education, reading just enough of the latest peer-reviewed studies to stay in practice but not nearly enough to become innovators or sought-after specialists or to optimize their skills. Teachers and professors, overwhelmed by course loads, administration, and the endless stream of papers that need grading, stop reading in the fields that used to fascinate them. I've also met more than a few attorneys who, while they do their best to represent their clients, routinely show up to court a little underprepared and never bother to sharpen their advocacy or negotiation skills. Spending thirty minutes of your Green Zone each day reading, studying, and honing your skills can make an astonishing difference. Like compound interest, the real benefits of small investments in your skill set show up years down the road.

But of course, most of us don't naturally live that way. When

the Stress Spiral sucks you in and you squeeze your most important work into the leftover space of your life, you cheat your gift.
You cheat your gift when you use it but never take the time to
develop it. And when you do that, you cheat the world out of
your best too.

You cheat your gift when you use it but never take time to develop it.

When you use your gift but never develop it, everybody loses.
You lose, because you never realize your potential. Your company
or organization loses, because they never get to fully leverage
your potential to further their mission. You lose in a third way,
because you end up wasting the best hours of your day—and
life—on things that don't really matter and that drain you (like
that breakfast meeting or emptying your inbox). Finally, working
outside of your gifting on a consistent basis is so demotivating it
can slide you into burnout.

Instead, imagine using your most productive hours to *develop*
your gift, not just use it. To really study and improve it until you
become the best you can be at what you do. A highly developed
skill set is what distinguishes the pros from everyone else. And
because you're doing something that as a rule you *love* to do,
those hours become synergistic. You end up more energized, not
less. Your energy and passion get renewed daily.

So, do the opposite of what most of us naturally do. Instead
of pushing your most important work and the work you're best at

into your Yellow and Red Zones—the desert of your work-week—do what you're best at when you're at your best.

That's your Green Zone. When you leverage it, my guess is it will become the most treasured hours of your day, whether you're at work or at home. The principles we cover in the rest of the book will show you how to refine it even more, but now you've got the key concepts. Mastering your Green Zone matters because, as Seneca noted in the quote that opened this chapter, "You must match time's swiftness with your speed in using it, and you must drink quickly as though from a rapid stream that will not always flow."[5] Your Green Zone is the most valuable time you've been given, and now you know what to do with it.

CHAPTER 5 IN A SNAP

- While you have twenty-four equal hours in a day, not all hours *feel* equal or *produce* equally. Leveraging your energy is where the exponential returns begin.
- A narrow gifting can be a superpower.
- Gifting + Passion + Impact = Optimal Green Zone Focus.
- Your *gifting* is what you're naturally good at.
- Your *passion is* what you love to do—what gives you energy.
- In the same way that not all hours are created equal, not all tasks are created equal.
- *Impact* refers to those things that, when done, make the biggest difference, sometimes in the moment but often in the long term.
- The more naturally gifted you are at something, the easier it is to spend *less* time on it, not more.
- You cheat your gift when you use it but never take the time to develop it.

- Use your most productive hours to *develop* your gift, not just use it.
- Your Green Zone, when leveraged, will become the most treasured hours of your day, whether you're at work or at home.

Use your most
productive hou

to _develop_ you
gift not just use *

→ read TW,
   study etc.

→ Ideas

YELLOW ZONE, RED ZONE, AND OTHER REAL-LIFE PROBLEMS

How to Leverage Non-Optimal Times and Situations

"I must be overtired," Buttercup managed. "The excitement and all."

"Rest, then," her mother cautioned. "Terrible things can happen when you're overtired. I was overtired the night your father proposed."

—William Goldman

Having spent your peak hours doing what you're best at, you might be asking, What about all the other hours?

Great question.

While we're at it, let me name something else you may be wondering about. Maybe you're thinking something like this: *Carey, this is awesome for you. But, unlike me, you're the boss—the senior leader of your organization. I don't have that kind of freedom at work, and besides, I have preschoolers. You got the Thrive Cycle up and running in your life when your kids were older, and now you're an empty nester, completely in control of your life and time. What about me?*

If you're asking questions like that, awesome. In this chapter we'll explore what to do with your Yellow and Red Zones and then clear up a few important questions about the circumstances that create energy challenges.

So, if you're ready to look at the rest of your day and deal with common questions and objections, let's dive in. We'll start with your Yellow and Red Zones, those non-optimal times you get every day that constitute the *majority* of your day. What do you do with those zones?

On the days when you've optimized your Green Zone, you'll be surprised at how productive and accomplished you feel. When your most important work is completed or well underway, it gives you a freedom you never enjoy otherwise, because the massive, important tasks that usually dangle in front of you into your evening hours are done. Or well underway. You used your Green Zone for them. The report is written. The meeting happened. The talk is ready for rehearsal. The new team member is hired. You already did what matters deeply, and now you're free to focus on the less demanding, less energizing tasks.

That takes a huge amount of pressure off the rest of the day, and as a result, everything else will feel less urgent and less important. But most days your to-do list can't be completed during your Green Zone, and there are hours yet to be put in. So, what do you do?

Simple: match the remaining tasks to your remaining energy zones.

YOUR YELLOW ZONE

Because your Yellow Zone consists of those hours when you have a moderate amount of energy, use those hours to do moderately important tasks.

Once you figure out what your most important tasks are and where your chief gifting and passions lie, you'll also be able to figure out what's moderately important and what's least important. You can probably just go back to your answers to the questions in the previous chapter and identify what didn't make the cut for your Green Zone.

I often hold meetings in my Yellow Zone. Sometimes the most critical connections make it into my Green Zone, but because producing quality content and clarifying strategy are some of my most important tasks, I rarely use my Green Zone for meetings. Yellow does just fine. During my Yellow Zone, I also work on calendar management with my staff and make decisions on what we'll do in the weeks and months ahead. I'm also a podcaster, and as important as my podcast is to my company, I'll do most interviews in my Yellow Zone because I have enough energy to complete the task well. Plus, it takes less effort for me to host a meaningful conversation than it does to create content from scratch.

YOUR RED ZONE

All of this leads us to your Red Zone, that time of day when you're running on your three remaining brain cells. Save your least important tasks for your Red Zone.

You might argue against that, thinking, *Well, won't I botch them?* Maybe. But if you're going to do a less-than-ideal job on some tasks, why not do it on the tasks that matter least, not the tasks that matter most? As you already know, if you waste your Green Zone or cheat your gift by not doing what you're best at when you're at your best, your Red Zone will sometimes get your most important work, which guarantees that you'll only *use* your gift, not *develop* it.

I use my low-energy zones to clear email, hold the lower-stakes meetings, do routine administrative work, and (increasingly) exercise. Years ago, I exercised in the morning. Since I wasn't training for a national cycling team, I realized using my peak hours to work out was probably a bad idea for me. These days, I usually do my workouts between 4:00 and 6:00 p.m.—my Red Zone. Even though I'm tired while getting my gear on and jumping on my bike, a sixty- to ninety-minute bike ride will completely reboot and reenergize my system. And it beats staring at a blinking cursor or falling asleep at my keyboard. If your employer is open to flexible hours (which a growing number are), starting early to get off early is an option, whether you're going to work out, take your kids to soccer practice, or do something else to redeem your lower energy zones.

The biggest Red Zone mistake you can make is to leave important decisions or critical tasks for this zone. On more than a few occasions, I've made decisions in my Red Zone, only to ask my assistant, two weeks later, who on earth made this boneheaded call. She then graciously reminded me it was me. Using your Red Zone to compose an email that's going out to the entire organization is a superb way to set yourself up to mistype "Let's take a shot at this" in front of thousands of people. (Don't ask me how I know this, but the *i* is next to the *o* on your keyboard.) Or try tackling conflict when you're exhausted. That always goes well.

You'll make optimal decisions in your Green Zone and good to great decisions in your Yellow Zone, but in your Red Zone, well, just don't tackle anything that really counts unless you have other people around to triple-check your work or watch your back in the meeting.

Again, you'll have to figure out how to match your exact responsibilities to your energy zones, but with a little experimentation, you'll find pairings that work well for you and for your organization.

So, now you've got a sense of how to use all three zones well. Before we leave this section of the book and move on to realizing your priorities, there are three real-world challenges worth addressing. As people discover their zones and start to implement the Thrive Cycle strategies, they consistently hit three roadblocks that are actually easy to overcome. Let's address them in turn.

CHALLENGE 1: I DON'T HAVE CONTROL OVER MY WORK CALENDAR

People often tell me the reason they can't use their three zones the way they want is because they're not in control of their work calendar in the same way other leaders are. It's a fair concern. Most employees and team members don't get to call the shots the way senior leaders, solopreneurs, and executives do.

That said, it's way too soon to throw in the towel.

You have more control over your calendar and life than you think. It doesn't feel that way because our minds instinctively gravitate to the things outside our control. In the same way it's easy to fixate on the weather when you're planning a day at the beach, it's natural to focus on the things you can't control at work: your unreasonable boss, the fact that it's crushingly busy, or any other factors you have little power over right now.

A much better approach is to flip that: to focus on what you *can* control, not on what you *can't*. And there's a surprising amount you *can* control.

Think about your week mathematically. Every week has 168 hours in it, and a typical workweek takes up about 40. That's it.

mathematics

You know what that amounts to, right? That means that you have complete control over 128 hours. Which in turn means that only 24 percent of the hours you'll spend in a given week are committed. That gives you 76 percent control.

While that's a little sobering, let's break down a 40-hour workweek even further.

Most office workers discover that meetings and other stated obligations usually amount to about 10 to 20 hours a week. As I've worked with thousands of leaders and asked them to drill down into their own workweeks, the majority are shocked to discover that there are usually only 10 to 12 hours of meetings or appointments they *have* to be in every week.

Any chance your total is about the same? If so, this means—are you ready?—the majority of even your work hours are probably within your control. If you have 20 hours of meetings and appointments that you can't change, that still means you have control over 88 percent of your week. Let that sink in for a minute.

YOUR WEEK

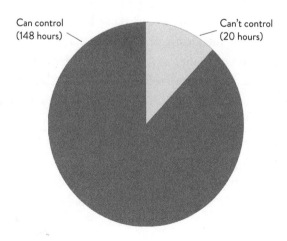

Can control
(148 hours)

Can't control
(20 hours)

Here's what's true (I had a hard time admitting this to myself, too, so I get it): you and your time are far less controlled by other people than you think. The real question becomes, So how much better can you do with the hours you *do* control?[1]

You and your time are far less controlled by other people than you think. So how much better can you do with the hours you do control?

While work may feel like it takes up all your life, you have remarkable freedom beyond it. You have 100 percent discretion over how you spend your non-working hours. Of course, you might argue that the kids have sports three nights a week and music lessons on two other nights. And there are meals to make and laundry to do, friends to see, not to mention sleep. All absolutely true. But realize that's all *your choice*. This is the life you built. I hope this book is helping you design a life you don't want to escape from. Coming to terms with how much freedom you actually have is part of that.

Again, you probably have control over at least 128 hours a week. Every week. And even if you have a side hustle around a passion project or are holding down two jobs to pay the bills, you have control over 110-plus hours each week. The question is, How can you restructure that time to make sure you're thriving? Not only will building margin and health into the rest of your week make your downtime better, but you'll also show up to work with a full tank rather than an empty one.

CHALLENGE 2: I'M NOT THE CEO

Another challenge the majority of people face at work is that they're not the CEO. I agree that being the senior leader gives you a built-in advantage, but having been a senior leader for decades now, I promise you that the position also comes with a unique set of stressors that almost offset the freedom you get (cue all the senior leaders who now nod their heads).

While the advantage of being the senior leader may not be as significant as you think, the question is fair: What do you do when you don't get to run the place and call the shots?

First, you've already seen that you probably have more freedom than you think. If you have 12 hours a week of scheduled meetings, you still have 156 hours when you're in charge. That's not a bad deal.

Next, look for any flex in your calendar where you can do what you're best at when you're at your best. Do your most important work when your energy is high, and shift all the low-importance activities to the Red Zone. If that means you have to come in early as a morning person or stay late if you're a night owl, most bosses don't object to people getting in early or staying late.

These shifts should renew your energy and help you become more effective.

Begin by shifting what you can, and then as you notice improvements, have a conversation with your boss to see whether other things could be changed.

Perhaps, with good reasons in each case, you could move one of your meetings from weekly to biweekly or reduce a ninety-minute meeting to a one-hour meeting. Sometimes it might be appropriate to ask to no longer attend a specific standing meeting or to come into the office occasionally on an as-needed basis and work remotely instead.

Shifting the times of meetings or commitments can also be helpful. Let's say you discover your weekly one-on-one with your supervisor is during a Red Zone. You could explain to him or her that you've been reading a book to try to become more effective at work and that you learned this is generally the time of day when you have the least energy. Asking him or her to move the meeting might be well received.

A few principles to follow when approaching your boss:

1. *Express desires, not demands.* Telling someone what you want him or her to do is far less effective than expressing what you'd love to see happen.
2. *Ask questions instead of making statements.* Phrasing your request as a question rather than a statement almost always helps you go further.
3. *Make sure you've done everything you can do.* You want to have maximized the factors within your control before you ask your leader about something beyond your control.[2]

A final word on this: Unless you have a completely irrational boss, your influence with your employer is highly dependent on the results you get for him or her. Be spectacularly good at what you do, and you might be surprised at how eager your employer is to make changes to accommodate you. And—remember— these changes are going to benefit your boss and your company as well, so that's double motivation for him or her to accommodate your requests.

CHALLENGE 3: I'VE GOT YOUNG KIDS OR A DIFFICULT FAMILY SITUATION

The final challenge that people run into happens when their home life isn't as stable or predictable as they wish it were. What if you have young kids or a newborn, for example? Or what if you're caring for aging parents or dealing with chronic health challenges in your family that require your care and attention? In those cases, is this advice just a pipe dream? Those are really weighty situations to address.

It's important that you adjust your expectations of what you can accomplish to your season of life. While there are some successful authors, podcasters, and speakers who have young kids at home (we met a few in the first chapter) or face challenging life situations, it might not be realistic or wise for you to set enormous goals for yourself if your free time is regularly spoken for. That's okay. Having a great family life and a strong marriage is an excellent goal. The advice in this book isn't just for people who want to launch something big; it's for people who want to do something meaningful and intentional with their lives, *whatever that means for them.* To get out of the Stress Spiral and live a fulfilling, healthy life while you care for others is a wonderful goal. You don't have to invent new forms of clean energy in your spare time.

One person told me that, given the special needs of his daughter, he felt like his whole life was a Yellow Zone. I empathize with that. Circumstances and even your own health can shrink your Green Zone and expand other zones for a season or chronically. Life comes at us in seasons and often with challenges we never asked for. But I hope the principles in this book can be adjusted to help you make the best of the situations you're dealing with.

I put these principles into practice when both of my sons were teenagers, and it transformed those years for me. Around the time of my burnout, my son Jordan (the musician)—who was then in ninth grade—asked me, "Dad, why can't you be like normal dads?" Always a great question to hear from your son.

I asked him what he meant by "normal dads."

"You know, normal dads are just around. They're not working all the time. They just hang out. They have time."

That's pretty good motivation to change your ways. So I canceled all my evening meetings for the next month and decided to be around.

The next day, as we finished dinner, I asked Jordan, "Hey, son, what do you want to do tonight? I'm around!"

"Uh . . . nothing, Dad. I'm going out with friends."

Teenagers.

You know what I learned in that moment, though? Being around is no guarantee that anything relationally significant will happen, but *not* being around is an absolute guarantee that nothing relationally significant will happen.

For the rest of his high school years, I was around a lot more as I put these principles into place. Same with my younger son.

I delayed some of my hopes and dreams for work because my deepest hopes and dreams were at home with my family. I didn't really start speaking on the road until I was forty. I didn't publish my first book until I was forty-four and my kids were in high school. I launched my podcast when I was forty-nine, and I didn't start traveling as widely as I do now until we became empty nesters and could do it together without leaving any kids behind.

I promise you, if you stay relatively healthy, there's a lot of life ahead of you after the kids leave home. If your situation is young kids or teenagers who need your love and attention, adjust your expectations and play the long game. It always pays off.

WHEN ALL ELSE FAILS, FOCUS ON THIS

I hope you find those adjustments and qualifications helpful. We'd all agree that life would be wonderful if it were 100 percent Green Zone. As awesome as that might be, even fasting intermittently and drinking coconut water won't make it so. No, you and I are living the real world of daily Yellow Zones and Red Zones, bosses who make unreasonable demands, nights of sleep lost to toddlers' nightmares, health concerns, the desire to care for others, and so many other challenges that make life what it is.

I struggle with my limits and the constraints life puts in my way. I get off course too. It's easy to howl at the moon and blame everyone and everything, and sometimes I still do that. But in my more sober moments, I'll come back to this one principle: focus on what you can control, not on what you can't.

There is so much within our control—from our bedtime, to our attitude, to what we eat and drink, to the sequence with which we tackle our work, to what we let slide and what we embrace. You have more control than you think. So do I. Mindset matters. As Henry Ford is quoted as saying, "Whether you believe you can do a thing or not, you're right."

Focus on what you can control, not on what you can't.

THINGS YOU LOVE AND THINGS YOU DON'T

Now that you've got a handle on your Green, Red, and Yellow Zones, spend some time on the exercise that follows. Review your learnings from this chapter and chapters 4 and 5, and categorize the tasks you need to tackle according to how much they energize you or drain you. Then use the chart on the next page to separate the things you love to do (and are gifted at) from the things you, well, don't love . . . and everything in between. Notice that the criteria for the list take into account both how you feel about the activity and its importance to you. Factoring in both will help you use your time more strategically.

With that in mind, use the Green Zone column for things that energize you, the Red Zone column for things that drain you, and the Yellow Zone column for everything in between. I've included my key tasks and priorities in a sample chart as an example. You'll see that exercise and email are in my Red Zone, but that doesn't mean they don't matter. They don't bring the highest value to my work, and I can easily do them when I'm not at my peak.

You don't have to get it perfect. Take your best shot at it. You can refer back to this list later as you block time for some of these core priorities on your calendar.

Once you've completed this exercise, we'll turn our attention to something that threatens to sabotage the days of even the most intentional leaders: hijacked priorities.

OPTIMAL ZONE PRIORITIES

GREEN	YELLOW	RED
ENERGIZING AND VERY IMPORTANT	MODERATELY ENERGIZING AND MODERATELY IMPORTANT	DRAINING AND LOW IMPORTANCE
Writing	Short-Term Projects	Email
Strategy	Calendar Management	Routine Meetings
Talk Preparation	Podcast Interviews	Expense Reports
	One-On-One and Team Meetings	Exercise

▼ Download your "Optimal Zone Priorities" worksheet at
www.AtYourBestToday.com

CHAPTER 6 IN A SNAP

- Do your moderately important tasks in your Yellow Zone, when you have a moderate amount of energy.

- Do your least important tasks in your Red Zone, when you have the least amount of energy.

- The biggest Red Zone mistake you can make is to leave important decisions or critical tasks for this zone.

- When you don't have complete control over your calendar, focus on what you *can* control, not on what you *can't*. And there's a surprising amount you *can* control.

- You and your time are far less controlled by other people than you think.

- Be spectacularly good at what you do, and you might be surprised at how eager your employer is to make changes to accommodate you.

- Being around is no guarantee that anything relationally significant will happen, but *not* being around is an absolute guarantee that nothing relationally significant will happen.

- "Whether you believe you can do a thing or not, you're right."

PART 4

REALIZE YOUR PRIORITIES

HIJACKED

Why It's So Easy to Fall Perpetually Behind

Hard choices, easy life. Easy choices, hard life.

—Jerzy Gregorek

Ever have one of those days you get excited about because there's nothing scheduled? No meetings. No video calls. Nothing but white space.

I love those unscheduled days too.

It's exciting. You can *finally* work for three undistracted hours on your research project. Or read a book that you've been meaning to crack. Or get deep into the numbers to produce the kind of analysis you know you're capable of. You can think. Breathe. Imagine. Dream.

And have you ever come to the end of one of those days only to discover that the entire day disintegrated? It just, well . . . Okay, you're not even sure what happened. All you know is that your optimal day of hyperproductivity blew up in your face. You didn't get anything done that you thought you would. The only thing you accomplished was to fall further behind.

THE ANATOMY OF A BAD DAY

Let's break down why that happens and why it keeps happening. To do that, we'll deconstruct one of my bad days as a leader and writer.

I start early because I want to get some good writing hours in before most people have breakfast. I head to my office before the sun rises, and first up on my writing list is a new article for my website, which also happens to mean I'm on the internet. Which leads to having a few tabs open that have nothing to do with anything I'm working on, which leads me to YouTube, where I watch a review of a laptop I want to buy to (ironically) make me more productive. As I glance at the browser tabs, I notice some unread emails. Turns out I missed a small fire that broke out last night on a project, so I try to put that out via email and then refocus.

Back to my article. As I scan the few words I've written, I remember I haven't finished my research, so I google some stats. As I type the insights into the post, two friends text me. Gotta reply to Frank. I always do.

Which reminds me I haven't posted to my social media accounts yet . . .

As I scroll, people start arriving in the office. Which, of course, is perfectly fine. I had set aside two more hours for writing, but they're not aware of that. So add some chitchat to the mix.

Sarah knocks on my door after nine o'clock and asks whether I have five minutes. I say I do, even though I don't feel like I do. And of course, five minutes becomes more than five minutes.

Twenty-three minutes later, I refocus, write for a bit, check email (again), and answer three more texts. A few more people ask for my time and input, and I'm invited to an impromptu early-afternoon meeting. Then I notice I'm hungry. It's lunchtime.

The meeting after lunch starts on time. I had budgeted an hour, but it runs late. After it's over, Justin asks me whether he can pick my brain on a project he's working on. One hour morphs into two hours plus.

I'm tired, so I duck out for a few minutes to grab a flat white and go for a short walk. I'm intercepted by a few more people as I meander back to my office. As I sit down, I see seventeen new emails. I dive into my inbox, and Sarah comes back with an update.

I plod through the emails and fresh texts, make a phone call, then go back to my original blog, only to notice it's now 4:17 p.m.

Sound familiar?

Welcome to almost every workday ever.

HOW YOUR PRIORITIES GET HIJACKED

What happened on that day is my priorities got hijacked. Just like yours do. And because we live in the real world, even when you embrace and master the Thrive Cycle, the human race, human nature, and gravity itself will conspire against you every day to thieve your productivity.

It's easy to blame everyone and everything else for my lack of productivity. But these days, I remind myself that everyone who calls, texts, knocks on my door, and asks me for things is just doing what every human being does: *trying to move his or her priorities onto my agenda.*

That's just the way life works. Nobody will ever ask you to

accomplish your top priorities. They will only ask you to accomplish theirs.

Think about it. Every text, every email, every random phone call, every knock on your door, every meeting you get invited to, every request you get puts other people's priorities on your calendar. Your friend is looking for advice, your coworker has a question, your neighbor needs help moving a desk up the stairs, and your toddler throws a temper tantrum. None of this is on your to-do list. One hundred percent of a workday or day off can be used up helping other people accomplish their priorities while yours sit unattended.

Nobody will ever ask you to accomplish your top priorities. They will only ask you to accomplish theirs.

Before you get mad at the world for this, just realize *that's exactly what you do too.* Most of the time when you interact with other people, you're attempting to hijack their priorities so you can accomplish yours. And the opposite phenomenon never happens. When was the last time someone texted or emailed you asking whether *you* had enough time to get your most important priorities accomplished that day? Or canceled a meeting just so you could breathe a little? Correct—*never.* Or at least rarely. Nor do you often do that for others.

What's made all this more complicated than it used to be in, say, 2007 (when the iPhone was introduced) is that you now carry a device in your pocket that gives the world access to you 24-7. Recently, when I was feeling particularly overwhelmed by the incessant number of requests coming my way, I counted something I'd never counted before—my inboxes.

I have eleven.

Yeah. I know. That's ridiculous. It's also true.

How, you ask, do I have eleven inboxes? Well, I have a few email addresses (public, private), but somebody decided that *every* social media platform should also have its own inbox and signed me up for that. Someone else at some very large tech company invented message *requests*. That way, someone who isn't connected directly with me on social media can send me a request to send me a message—just one more fun little stream of inbound communication to deal with.

My guess is you have more inboxes than you think too. Count 'em. They help explain your paralysis.

There are so many ways to get ahold of you digitally—and so many ways to get distracted—that peace remains elusive. Everywhere you turn, every moment of the day, people have access to you. Even when you're in the bathroom, people message you. And even when you're eating or trying to go to sleep, the onslaught continues.

THE MYSTERY THAT ISN'T A MYSTERY

If you look at it honestly, the "oh my goodness, what happened to my day?" phenomenon you and I experience is not really a mystery. You simply spent your day reacting to everything that came your way.

That's exactly how your priorities get hijacked. That's how you work all day and accomplish nothing—or at least nothing you planned to do. It's why the most important things you're tasked with are the very things that don't get done. It's also why you're so exhausted and overwhelmed. Getting frustrated day after day after day because nothing *you* want to get done gets done, well, that's not a great way to live, especially when you have significant things to do.

You can get time and energy working in your favor, but unless you get priorities working in your favor, too, all you have is a fun new rhythm and a nifty theory that remains theoretical.

To overcome the perpetual hijacking, you need a strategy, which is what we'll explore in detail next.

Your priorities get hijacked in three significant ways: by tasks you didn't prioritize strategically, by your own tendency to get distracted (I am *so* guilty of this), and of course, by people. We'll devote a chapter to each of these challenges.

Let's start with prioritizing the right tasks. Although we touched on tasks in chapter 5 to help sort out which basic tasks are most important for you to focus on, let's break that down even further so you get far more done in even less time.

THE WRONG THINGS ALWAYS WANT YOUR ATTENTION

On a typical day, the wrong things eat up most of your attention. Stephen Covey has helpfully pointed out the distinction between things that are urgent and things that are important.[1] His categories are worth revisiting here.

Covey pointed out that some things are neither urgent nor important. That wormhole you went down on YouTube is a good example. Sure, the first video was intentional, but the sixteen others, less so, particularly the really cool #fail video featuring skiers who ended up in body casts. Social media, gaming, chit-chat in the office, and random texts and phone calls make life interesting, but they don't help you accomplish your goals. When you audit your life honestly, it is amazing to realize how much productive time gets spent on things that are neither important nor urgent.

Continuing with Covey's categories, some things are urgent but not important: a random knock on your door, that friend from high school who texted you about nothing in particular but still wants a reply, or the meeting that's on the calendar but accomplishes little. You really can't skip it, but . . . This category includes everything that feels urgent but ultimately doesn't matter much.

Next, Covey said, are the things that are truly urgent *and* important—like putting out a kitchen fire, for example, or preparing for a court hearing tomorrow, taking a call from your boss, or hitting the deadline for your annual meeting.

Finally, Covey said there are the things that are important but not urgent. This is the category that drives most of your frustration and regret. Important but not urgent priorities include exercise, goal setting, developing your gift, personal financial planning, book reading, spiritual development, emotional health (get thee to a therapist), playtime with your kids, or even a date night with your spouse. It's so easy to let any or all of these things slide.

What makes it more complicated is that you never pay an immediate price for skipping important but non-urgent things. The cost is always long term. Worse, the price only gets steeper the longer you ignore them. You pay now. Or you pay way more later.

So, let's get brutally honest for a moment. If you *really* had to audit your days, how much of what you spend your time on is neither urgent nor important?

Cue the awkward silence.

Yup. Way. Too. Much.

All this stuff that *wasn't* on your list got done. The real value—your best work, your greatest contribution—got squashed, ignored, deferred, or squeezed in. Almost all the things left undone are important but not urgent.

The wrong things will always want your attention. It's your job to focus on the right things. The question, of course, is, How do you do that? While the next few chapters are devoted to helping you realize your priorities, three things can help you start making real progress. Think of these as metashifts that will reorient how you think about priorities. In the next two chapters, we'll work through some specific strategies and tactics that will help you optimize each of your three zones and accomplish what's most important to you. The first big shift that will help you make progress is to even further refine your focus.

NARROWING YOUR FOCUS

When everything either seems important or presents itself as important, how do you know what really matters most?

As you may know, years ago, Italian engineer, sociologist, economist, political scientist, and philosopher Vilfredo Pareto observed that 80 percent of the effects come from 20 percent of the causes. Pareto detected this trend in land ownership, noting that in nineteenth-century Italy 80 percent of the land was owned by 20 percent of the population. This principle was quickly observed by others in many fields, from economics (80 percent of the profit is produced by 20 percent of the products) to exercise (80 percent of the gains in performance are produced by 20 percent of the exercises).

Applied to your time use and mine, the principle would suggest that most people spend 80 percent of their time on the things that produce 20 percent of their results, which we'd all agree is probably a bad idea. If you really want to see exponential spikes in productivity and results, flip it. Expand the time you spend on high-yield activities. The goal, then, becomes to spend 80 percent of your time on the 20 percent of activities and tasks that produce 80 percent of your results.

As the founder of a leadership company, I've realized that our team and the leaders we serve have the most success when I focus on five things:

- casting crystal-clear vision
- creating and delivering great content
- crafting a healthy organizational culture
- keeping our top staff and clients aligned and relationally connected
- ensuring we have the financial resources we need for our mission

As any leader knows, there are about eighty-six other things I could spend my time on, but these five produce the greatest results. This has become a filter for me to use to sift through all the requests that come my way. If it's not directly related to one of these five things, it usually doesn't make my calendar. Back when I was leading a church full time, the only thing that was different was that the content I was creating centered on weekly sermons. Everything else? Pretty much the same: clear vision, healthy culture, a team that is aligned and connected, and financial health.

In your personal life, you can also find a few things that move the needle more than anything else. Before my kids went to college, being at home for dinner, attending their events and activities, going on a weekly date with my wife, and spending evenings home and "around" made for the best results at home. Now that

I'm an empty nester, I prioritize having at least one sit-down meal and lingering conversation every day with my wife, traveling together, going on weekly dates, and doing activities we love together (boating, hiking, cycling, spending time with friends) as well as seeing our grown kids and family regularly. Personally, a full night's sleep (I get seven to eight hours every night), regular exercise, and starting my day before sunrise with an hour of prayer, Scripture reading, and reflection make the biggest difference.

If you were to show up and shadow me for a week, what I've outlined in the preceding paragraphs is basically what I now spend 80 percent of my work time and personal time doing. It's not fancy or flashy, but my goodness, it's rewarding.

Notice that, for the most part, these important priorities aren't urgent. I could skip almost all of them, and few people would complain. But these are the things that give my life and leadership meaning, purpose, and sustainability. This explains why you're so frustrated day after day and why you may feel like you're not accomplishing enough meaningful things with your life. Hopes and dreams get pushed off day after day, which as you know, in no time becomes year after year. All because urgent but ultimately unimportant things used up your best time and energy.

So, my question to you is, What are the 20 percent of things you do that produce 80 percent of the results? This is a critical question to answer because it will help you further refine how you should spend your Green Zone time. When you spend 80 (or 100) percent of your Green Zone on the things that produce 80 percent of your results, your ability to accomplish significant things soars in your life and in your leadership.

MASTERING THE ART OF THE CLEAR NO

The strategy we've covered so far—and much of what follows—will compel you to say the one thing most of us really dislike saying: no. So many people I know are people pleasers, and that's my leaning too. Without a strategy for saying no, you default to yes, and your life vaporizes with other people's priorities being realized rather than yours.

Public service announcement: the art of saying no is *not* easy. I've learned to say no as a matter of discipline, but my heart still leans toward yes. Stop me in the hall at an event I'm speaking at and ask me to go for coffee, and unless you haven't showered in five days or you tell me how much you hate what I do, everything in me will want to go to coffee with you. (And even if you told me you hate what I do, I'd be curious enough to try to figure out why . . . so let's grab coffee. Maybe I'm missing something.)

Without a strategy for saying no, you default to yes, and your life vaporizes with other people's priorities being realized rather than yours.

You know that saying no to good things allows you to say yes to great things, but you cave again and say yes to a stupid meeting, which causes you to show up way too late to your son's football game.

As Steve Jobs famously noted, "People think focus means saying *yes* to the thing you've got to focus on. But that's not what it means at all. It means saying *no* to the hundred other good ideas that there are. You have to pick carefully. I'm actually as proud of the things we haven't done as the things I have done. Innovation is saying *no* to 1,000 things."[2]

Why are we so afraid of saying no? You're probably afraid of disappointing people, coming off like a jerk, or both. So let me give you in a few pages something that took me years to develop and get good at: a clear, simple strategy for how to say no (nicely).

1. Tell them you'd love to meet with them. That's probably the truth. In a perfect world, you likely would love to meet with them. And that's a great, honest place to start. So start there . . . but don't stop there. Keep moving through the next steps.

2. Express empathy. Empathy defuses tension. Let them know you understand where they're coming from. You're on their side and want to be helpful even if you can't meet with them.

3. Be firm. Even when you express it with kindness, make sure your answer is direct. Let them know that as much as you'd love to meet, you're not going to. Saying no sounds like this:

- "In order to honor my other commitments, I'm going to decline."
- "As much as I'd love to, I'm afraid I'm not in."
- "I'm so sorry. That's not going to work."
- "I'm not available."
- "Thank you, but I'm going to pass."

What unites all these variations is they're all clear. There's no false hope. It's just no. Providing a reason isn't necessary, but it can help to say something like "in order to honor my current commitments" or "because I have to focus on this next project" or "for the foreseeable future I just don't see how I can make this work."

None of us can do it all. Remind yourself that you can't prioritize the people who matter most to you if you say yes to everyone else.

4. Redirect them. Maybe you can't help them, but someone else might be able to. If there's someone better suited to help them or another organization (or even a competitor) who would be better, send them there. This shift in the focus from you to whom they really need or want will serve them just as well or better.

5. Thank them. Even though you say no to the requests, honor the relationships. Let them know how much you appreciate them simply for asking and how grateful you are for them. Here's what that sounds like (written or said with a smile on your face):

- "But thank you so much for asking. I really appreciate you and all you're doing."
- "That was so kind of you to invite me. Thank you, and I'm sorry it won't work out."
- "I appreciate the invite. I'm really grateful for you and all you're doing. Thank you."

I recently experienced a great example of a firm no that felt just fine when I asked a friend who leads a large and influential organization to be a speaker at an event I was planning. I texted him with the request, and later in the day he called me. After asking some questions, he said, "I'm going to say no to this one, but I appreciate you asking me." He explained why and then affirmed he'd like to do something in the future. We talked for another forty-five minutes about the future, leadership, and common goals. When I finally hung up, as much as I would have appreciated a yes, the no didn't sting at all. I respected him more for it. And it reminded me, once again, that scarcity creates value.

See? You don't have to be a creep. You can still be friends.

When you're tempted to cave, remind yourself that because time is a limited commodity, saying yes to something good now will lead you to say no to something great later.

If you're still a little uncomfortable with saying no, you're not alone. I have a free download for you with several text, email, and verbal scripts you can use to tell people no (nicely). Think of it as a free "How to Say No (Nicely)" cheat sheet.

▼ Download the "How to Say No (Nicely)" cheat sheet at
www.AtYourBestToday.com

MAKING CATEGORICAL DECISIONS

If mastering the art of saying no seems appealing, wait until you master categorical decision-making. Categorical decision-making is making one decision that eliminates dozens or hundreds of other decisions.

Strangely (and tragically), the fastest introduction to categorical decision-making for all of us happened in March 2020 when the world shut down because of the coronavirus pandemic.

People will remember for decades what they were doing as the world stopped and our individual worlds closed down. So much of what was normal life for all of us disappeared overnight. If you look back on your life, whole categories of events, rhythms, and rituals ceased almost instantly. All kinds of things that had been options suddenly weren't.

For years prior to COVID-19, my team and I had debated how much I should be on the road speaking at events. The consensus was I was probably on the road too much and I needed to cut back. But the opportunities were many and, well, attractive. We had eliminated some kinds of speaking engagements categorically (subjects I no longer spoke to, types of audiences I generally no longer spoke to), but it still left us on the edge of how much I should accept. The week the world shut down, I was scheduled to speak at SXSW in Austin, Texas, followed almost immediately by a five-city speaking tour of Australia. Flights, hotels, and rides were booked. As the virus spread across America and around the world, I was on the phone and email daily, trying to figure out what to do. Within a matter of hours, the questions over whether to go or not go disappeared when SXSW canceled its 2020 event, governments around the world closed their borders, and the world as we knew it ground to a halt.

For me it wasn't just two speaking trips that were canceled. A year of speaking events disappeared or switched to virtual. Talk about categorical decision-making. For a person who was used to hopping flights and navigating time zones multiple times a week, speaking in person was suddenly off the table indefinitely. Decision made. A whole category of activity in my life closed instantly.

When you think about the categories of things that disappeared from your life overnight —working from an office, the commute, school, parties, shopping, church, sports, weddings, other gatherings, vacations, visits with friends—it reminds you that as much as you wanted to bring all or most of these things back into your life, you had the power to radically redefine what you do and what you don't do. That moment showed me afresh what can happen when you simply stop doing entire categories of things.

That's the power of categorical decision-making. While COVID-19 was involuntary and cruel, removing entire categories of things from your calendar and life to liberate your priorities is a wonderful voluntary practice as well.

The typical response to being overwhelmed is to try to cut something—*anything*—out of your calendar temporarily.

Your first impulse (and mine) is to try to fix the problem with ad hoc, temporary solutions, such as these:

- "Free up my afternoon."
- "Cancel all my meetings next week."
- "Tell Trevor I just can't do July. September, maybe."
- "Let's change our plans next weekend."
- "Could I take a week off at the end of the month?"

While this provides a bit of relief, the challenge with this kind of approach is that it provides a temporary, isolated solution to a more systemic problem. The system you built on the fly is broken, and temporary relief is only going to delay the problem.

Categorical decision-making eliminates groups of people or things from your calendar and life. Here are some practical examples of categorical decisions you can make:

- Eliminate particular kinds of meetings. For example, stop doing breakfast meetings, lunch meetings, meetings over one hour, evening meetings, or weekend meetings.
- Change the levels of one-on-one meetings that you personally do as your company grows. Perhaps you no longer

meet with all employees but just with managers, the leadership team, or the executive team.

- No longer allow people to meet "for no reason" or simply "to pick your brain." Or limit these to one a month, as in, "March is already full, but I have one opening in April."
- Pick one to three charities you support generously, which makes saying no to all other requests automatic. "Thanks for asking. We already have our giving commitments selected for this year."
- On the personal front, decide which kinds of invitations you accept and which you don't. One friend of ours, early in her marriage and motherhood, decided not to accept budget-threatening multilevel-marketing "parties" for things like essential oils, makeup, or kitchen gadgets. She just told her friends, "I don't go to parties like that, but I'm happy to get together for coffee when you're free."
- Create guidelines about audience composition. For example, in the early days, I spoke almost anywhere I was invited. These days, I speak only to leaders, not to general audiences. The rationale? Speaking to a group of five hundred leaders (or in some cases, even fifty or five) can have far more long-term impact than speaking to a large audience of randomly assembled people.

This automates your decision-making not just for you but also for your team or family. You've predecided what you will do and won't do.

Deciding what you won't do ahead of time will free you to do what you want to do in the moment. It becomes so much easier to eliminate overwhelm when you have categories you've simply eliminated. And you avoid all the mental floundering—time and energy—involved in thinking about whether you should say yes or no.

Categorical decision-making is one of the easiest ways to free up space on your calendar, including the time you save by not having to make a dozen or a hundred decisions about what you've now eliminated.

BUT YOU'RE AFRAID OF MISSING OUT

The greatest fear you'll likely encounter with this step is the fear of missing out. What if you miss out on an amazing opportunity? Aren't there exceptions to the rule? What if everything doesn't fit into a neat and tidy category?

If something that you feel you should say yes to comes along, say yes. Because you've already eliminated ninety-nine things that would not have been the best use of your time in that category, you can say yes to the one or two things that are the exceptions to the rule. And if you made a category delineation that isn't working for you (it's accurate only, say, 50 percent of the time), rethink your category or nuance it so it serves you better.

You don't have to be elitist either. I believe one mark of great leadership is to help people who probably can't help you back. So take the time to do that for no other reason than it's the right thing to do. Do an event that doesn't fit your normal profile, and decide to do it for free. Or you may leave a spot open strategically to meet with entry-level employees or clients. Most of the great CEOs and other leaders I know do just that.

The point is, you can be strategic about your decisions to be charitable with your time and energy. You can't have your calendar filled with non-priorities if you want to accomplish what you're most called to accomplish.

Categorical decision-making saves mental energy and a tremendous amount of time because you already made the decision. Case closed. Move on.

When you decide what you won't do, it frees up time and energy to fulfill your purpose.

So fear not.

YOUR NEXT HIJACKER IS...

We covered a lot in this chapter. These three shifts—narrowing your focus, mastering the art of saying no, and making categorical decisions—are the first part of the strategy to stop the hijacking of your priorities.

But before you declare the hostage-taking over, there are two other areas to focus on to truly liberate your priorities. The next hijacker is, well, you.

CHAPTER 7 IN A SNAP

- Everyone who calls, texts, knocks on your door, and asks you for things is just doing what every human being does: trying to move his or her priorities onto someone else's agenda.

- Nobody will ever ask you to accomplish your top priorities. They will only ask you to accomplish theirs. Frankly, you do the same thing.

- Most people spend their day reacting to everything that comes their way.

- The wrong things will always want your attention.

- Spend 80 percent of your time on the things that produce 80 percent of your results.

- Saying no to good things allows you to say yes to great things. Ironically, saying yes to something good now will lead you to say no to something great later.

- Categorical decision-making is the art of making one decision that eliminates dozens or hundreds of other decisions.

- Deciding what you won't do frees up time and energy for the things you will do and want to do.

CHAPTER 8

DISTRACTION-FREE

How to Stop Interrupting Yourself

The greatest weariness comes from work not done.

—Eric Hoffer

How often do you think you touch your phone in a day?

Fun fact.

One study shows that average people touch their smartphones 2,617 times a day. Let that sink in for a minute . . . That's *two thousand and six hundred seventeen* times a day.

And those are *average* users.

Heavy users touch their phones 5,427 times a day.[1] Yikes.

I'm now officially averting my eyes in shame. I'm a recovering heavy user. I don't need to touch my phone that often, but left to my own devices, I do (see what I did there?).

Think for a minute about the implication of living with that level of distraction and interruption from technology. It's staggering.

To wrap your brain around it, imagine that the notifications on your phone and various other devices, instead of being buzzes, chirps, rings, or dings, came from a human who rang your front doorbell. Every time there's a message or notification, there's a dude at your front door instead.

So, you're working away, doing some deep research, and the doorbell rings.

You get up from your desk, hobble down the stairs, and open the door. The human text messenger says, "What do you want for lunch?" A bit annoyed, you force a smile and tell him, "A turkey avocado ciabatta sandwich, please."

You thank him, close the door, and head back toward the stairs.

The doorbell rings again.

You roll your eyes, spin around, head back to the door, and swing it open.

"Mayo?"

And so it continues all day.

If notifications on your phone were human beings, that's exactly what your life would be like.

It's funny how we would never accept that many interruptions from people (that's why they issue restraining orders), but somehow we tolerate it with technology and other things that hijack our priorities. When technology runs us, it can ruin us. Technology makes a wonderful servant but a terrible master.

In this chapter, we'll explore how to combat the distractions that come at you when you're trying to work productively. Our devices are one thing, but if you're like me, you don't even really need an enemy to interrupt you. You have one. It's a perpetually distracted you. I can interrupt myself and get off track all by myself.

You don't need an enemy to interrupt you. You have one. It's a perpetually distracted you.

As Nir Eyal pointed out in *Indistractable,* the opposite of distraction isn't focus. The opposite of distraction is *traction,* which comes from a Latin word meaning "to draw or pull," like a tractor, horse, or truck pulls things forward.[2] To put it simply, the reason you don't have traction on the goals and priorities you've set for yourself is that you often get distracted.

PAY ATTENTION

Distraction is *expensive.* That truth is reflected in the expression we use when we try to get someone refocused: "Pay attention!" Even attention *deficit* disorder (which, although never officially diagnosed, I think I have) implies that your attention is limited and easily runs amok.

To make matters more interesting, we live in the era of the attention economy—a concept developed by psychologist, economist, and Nobel laureate Herbert A. Simon to describe the competition for our attention.[3] All day long, companies and people vie for your attention—from sensationalist news headlines, to the algorithms that online media companies design to keep you engaged longer, to email subject lines cleverly crafted to stand out, to this book's cover, which has been an apparently successful attempt to capture your attention. And continuing to capture your attention is also what I'm trying to do with these words right now.

Every time you give your attention to something or someone, it *costs* you. Invested well, attention can pay big dividends—from a family that's close knit, to a book that changes your life, to a breakthrough idea.

However—and this is the point—much of your attention and mine gets captured by things that really don't matter. Paying attention to the wrong things costs you. It costs you your priorities. Your goals. Your productivity. Your health. It can even cost you your family. Let it wander long enough, and eventually it costs you your potential and your dreams.

Researchers have discovered that it takes the average person almost twenty-five minutes to refocus after a single distraction.[4] Wow. Twenty-five minutes every time someone asks you, "Mayo?" If you've ever said "Now, where was I?" or "What was that idea again?" you know exactly what I'm talking about. Sometimes you get those ideas back. Sometimes you don't.

As Cal Newport argued, the ability to do deep work in our distracted culture is both increasingly rare and increasingly valuable. The opposite of deep work, Newport said, is shallow work. Shallow work is "noncognitively demanding, logistical-style tasks, often performed while distracted."[5] Your Yellow and Red Zones are great places for that. And there is, inevitably, shallow work in all our lives. But your Green Zone? That's something worth protecting and optimizing.

So, how do you guard your attention? Particularly when you're in your Green Zone, where deep work pays off most? Further optimizing your Green Zone has an awful lot to do with *where* you spend your Green Zone.

YOUR BEST ENVIRONMENT

So we've covered what to do to optimize your productivity and when to do it. Now's it's time to tackle where you do it. In the same way that not all *hours* are created equal and not all *tasks* are created equal, not all *environments* are created equal. Some of my best friends *love* working in coffee shops. They love the background noise and the constant movement of people. I just can't produce anything of quality in that environment.

Optimal environments can vary from personality type to personality type and person to person. The test is that it just has to work for you. The best thing you can do to discover your optimal environment is to become a student of yourself. That might take some experimentation, and to do that, you can begin with this question: Where do you produce your best work?

To some extent, we humans are like plants when it comes to our productivity: we need the right ecosystem to help us thrive. Various factors affect a plant's health and ability to flourish: soil conditions, moisture, light levels, humidity. A cactus flourishes in a hot, arid climate. That climate would kill a petunia or Kentucky bluegrass. Similarly, a hot, humid environment that a bird-of-paradise loves would rot a cactus.

What are your ideal conditions? Can you access them as often as possible during your best three to five hours a day?

My favorite place for focused work is on my porch at home. Any idea what your ideal space might be? A corner of a spare bedroom or basement family room you can carve out for your-self? A nook at the end of a hallway? I know one leader who converted his garage to his sacred space to do deep work.

Quiet space for deep work matters. To generate activity takes little thought. But to distill meaning, discern purpose, connect ideas, spot trends, solve problems, or fix a system that is deeply broken, well, that requires careful thought. And ample time. Everything that interrupts you and distracts you competes with that. The place where you work matters.

So, here's my plea, regardless of your personality type: find or create the most undistracted environment you can for your Green Zone. As you search for the right physical space, think beyond design and privacy. Remember to consider things like temperature (is it too hot or too cold to focus?), lighting (too bright or too dim?), and even noise. Not just outside noise, but pesky little things like the buzz from an old fluorescent light.

Feel free to take radical measures and even appear antisocial—your focus matters that much. Mark Twain may have lived in a quieter century, but he did his writing in a cabin on his property so he could be completely undistracted for hours at a time. His family, the story goes, used a horn to let him know that meals were ready, so deep was his concentration. Fast-forward to our day, and writers from J. K. Rowling to Donald Miller still seques-ter themselves to do their work. With the shift to working from home taking place in our culture, many people have carved quiet workspaces out of guest rooms, basements, and even closets.

Since I live in Canada, my porch works for me only about five to six months a year. Then I retreat to an office in my basement, where, one floor beneath the world, I have my books, a simple, clean walnut desk, some white paneled walls, a few favorite chairs, a barn door that cordons me off from the rest of the house, and a chance to sink deep into thought and work.

You may not have access to a writer's cabin, but you do need to focus deeply and for sustained periods (think hours, not minutes) to produce the best work you're capable of, whether that's a breakthrough idea, an innovative strategy, a killer report, more beautiful code, a new approach to leading people, a fresh slide deck, or a finished manuscript.

WHAT IF YOU CAN'T GET OPTIMAL?

Thanks for hanging in there while I painted an ideal picture. And trust me—it's more realizable than you think, even if it ends up being a corner in a spare bedroom or your garden shed.

But I get it. You and I live in the real world. Coworkers, friends, and family have a habit of invading even the most sublime workspaces. Your neighbor might start mowing her lawn just as your best idea is dawning on you. The construction workers down the road never ask you whether this is a good time to use the jackhammer. Or you might have to go to work every day and sit in your assigned cubicle.

So, does that mean you just can't optimize your Green Zone? Well, no. Optimal conditions are a *goal,* not a requirement. If you're waiting for perfect conditions to do your best work, you'll wait forever.

Because of the typical level of travel in my life, I often kiss my porch and basement retreat goodbye. I've had to learn to adapt to hotel rooms, green rooms, lobbies, airports, and planes, where noise-canceling headphones (also known as people-canceling headphones) have become my best friend. By the way, headphones are a fantastic idea for productivity, even when you're working in your cubicle or in a hotel lobby while waiting for check-in. Note: you don't have to listen to anything. Just having them on emits the almost-universal signal of "Dude, don't bug me."

Some leaders put signs on their doors or traffic cones on their desks to indicate that they're not available right now. Healthy colleagues respect boundaries like that.

Maximizing your Green Zone with an optimal work environment requires constant innovation and flexing. It's summer as I'm writing this, and my wife and I are on a working vacation (bad idea, but hey, deadlines) at a lodge on a gorgeous lake a few hours north of Toronto. Sounds perfect, right?

Well, nope. The lodge is busy, and the beach has lots of people on it (many of whom I know), so I've taken off to the middle of the lake, where I'm writing all alone on the bow of a boat.

Similarly, travel, sleepless nights, crises, hosting friends and guests, and other situations will pop up on a semiregular basis. That's called life. Obviously, to the extent you can control these things, move them out of your Green Zone. But you're not a machine. You're human. You won't be able to optimize your Green Zone every day. I don't. Don't beat yourself up. When you run into surprises and obstacles, focus on what you *can* control, not on what you *can't*.

Renowned writer Vladimir Nabokov didn't let circumstances limit his output. When his tiny flat didn't have room for a desk, he decided to write in the bathtub.[6] If Nabokov could pen novels next to a toilet, you and I can probably find some arrangement that works too.

So, what kind of environment can you find to cultivate your best work? Do it. Get focused deeply enough to produce your best work. Spend as much Green Zone time in optimal conditions as possible. And when you can't, simply do your best.

Just know this. When you do what you're best at when you're at your best in the best conditions you can create, your work comes alive. And so do you.

When you do what you're best at when you're at your best in the best conditions you can create, your work comes alive. And so do you.

TURN OFF ALL NOTIFICATIONS

Wherever you spend your Green Zone, you will still experience interruptions. Most will be digital. One of the best ways to protect your Green Zone is to turn off all notifications on all your devices. Notifications, of course, are those things that make your device buzz, chirp, ring, and ding with updates: breaking news, text notifications, email notifications, social media updates, and on and on.

Almost everything in the digital universe will try to convince you to keep those notifications on. After all, everything and everyone is vying for your attention. It's how a lot of companies make their money, and they're good at it. Instead, give them your attention on *your* schedule, not theirs. Notifications push you to do the opposite: access content on *their* schedules, not yours.

The default settings of most apps and devices is to have notifications enabled. It takes only a few minutes to disable all notifications on your phone, tablet, and computer. Those few minutes will save you literally days or weeks in productivity each year. I also set all my devices to Do Not Disturb. That means virtually nothing gets through while I'm working or when I'm off and hanging out with friends and family.

I can imagine that at this point you're thinking, *But I'll miss all my texts, phone calls, and other important notices.* And the answer to that is "Correct. That's the point."[7]

You can program some people to break through your Do Not Disturb wall, and I do that for family, close team members, and my best friends. But doing it for ten is different from doing it for everyone. If my wife or kids call, they get through. They usually text, so if they call, I know it's exceptionally urgent.

While shutting the world off for a few hours can create a small panic inside you, try it. Start with one day and see what happens. Here's what I imagine you'll discover. You haven't totally *disabled* communication. All those messages and other things you missed are still there waiting for you when you're ready to engage them. You really haven't missed a thing. All you've done is decided to control when you reply.

Still worried about missing really important stuff? If it truly is an emergency, the police or fire department will knock at your door and let you know that something happened. Until then, enjoy the free headspace and productivity that come with the quiet. Most things that present themselves as urgent aren't urgent.

TAKE A WALK

Now that you've found your best three to five hours and you're in the best environment for deep work—or at least the best spot you can find—and your notifications are off so you can stay focused, what do you do? You might think you should power through your to-do list until there's nothing left. And some days that might be the best thing you can do.

But if you're going to *develop* your gift, not just *use* it, and work *on* your business, not just *in* your business, the best idea is to do what you never do when you spend all day powering through your list—harness the mind-body connection.

It's tempting to think that once you're in your Green Zone, you need to keep your fingers locked on a keyboard, your pen attached to paper, or your key people moving in and out of your office until your work is done. Sometimes that is exactly what you need to do with your Green Zone.

But often it's not, especially if you're going to do the very best work you're capable of. The quality of your work is determined by the quality of your thinking. And high-quality thinking is incompatible with constant output.

On a regular basis during your Green Zone, give yourself time to breathe. Get up from your chair while you ponder ideas. Read a book that challenges your thinking. Go through three drafts of your project, not just two. Research, reflect, work through a few versions, dream, consult, and then tackle it again. Study, imagine, rethink, polish, and develop multiple iterations.

And don't be afraid to *really* relax and block space. Although I generally exercise in my Red Zone, if I'm working on really fresh ideas or need to generate a breakthrough, I'll sometimes include physical activity in my Green Zone. Neuroscience increasingly shows that physical activity (walking, running, cycling) allows the subconscious mind to generate better ideas. This is why, stereotypically, you have some of your best ideas in the shower. It's when your mind isn't intentionally engaged that your subconscious spits out the solution to the problem you were trying to solve two days before.

Apple cofounder Steve Jobs was famous for his walks. When I visited Palo Alto for the first time a few years ago, I found the house Steve lived in. It's located in a beautiful tree-lined neighborhood. I parked my car on the street, and my wife, Toni, and I spent an hour walking through the neighborhood. It was tremendously relaxing and beautiful. The trees were mature and the gardens manicured. I could see why Steve often coerced his colleagues into taking long walks through the neighborhood to produce ideas. I'm not sure you stumble on the idea of a thousand songs in your pocket by simply sitting behind a computer all day in an office or talking in a boardroom.

The philosopher Friedrich Nietzsche, who also walked every day, wrote that "only thoughts which come from *walking* have any value." So, in your Green Zone, as necessary, walk, run, ride, bike, saunter, and wander to generate ideas, and see what happens. You'll be surprised.

EARLY MORNINGS: ONE MORE KILLER ADVANTAGE

You know your Green Zone hours, and maybe you've made peace with them, but before we leave the subject of distraction and focus, I need to ask a question that always sparks debate and always annoys non-morning people. The question: Do morning people have an advantage over everyone else?

My answer? I think they do.

My bias for mornings comes in part from my current wiring as an early riser but also from a conviction that early mornings carry an advantage no other time of day does: the rest of the world is still asleep. While you should still turn off all notifications and silence your devices no matter when your Green Zone lands on the clock, the reality is, between 5:00 and 8:00 a.m., nobody's going to text you. No one's knocking at your door, emailing you, or otherwise trying to get your attention. The world is hushed, and the rush of the workday and school day hasn't started.

5 – 8:00
Am

Early mornings can be especially productive, not because you don't notice the distractions but because those distractions aren't there in the first place. Which usually means you can get things done faster and better, because focusing becomes so much easier.

It's a bit like traffic. If you live in the country and have to drive thirty miles to work, you end up with a thirty-minute commute. If you live in Los Angeles, traveling thirty miles to work is more like a ninety-minute drive—or worse. The only difference is the number of other people trying to do the same thing at the same time. Same distance. Big difference.

When the world is loud and everyone's trying to do what you're trying to do, it's just that much harder to focus, and most people make far less progress. Which means if you can get yourself up early enough, leveraging the hours before the world gets moving can be a serious advantage. For me it's been life giving. Imagine getting your best work and thinking done before other people eat their breakfast.

Whether you wake up early or not, if you really want to thrive during the day and make every zone better, make sure you get enough sleep. I realize I sound like your mom, but it's becoming clear that sleep is a secret weapon. I have prioritized rest postburnout in a way I never did before my crash, and I'm shocked at how much better I routinely feel. Pro athletes are also realizing that the amount of recovery and rest time they take is directly connected to their ability to perform at peak levels. LeBron James sometimes sleeps ten hours a night, and if he doesn't get enough rest, he'll make time for a nap, realizing that the intense energy and focus he brings to the court are things his rest and recovery fuel.[9] When I interviewed LA Lakers' general manager Rob Pelinka for my leadership podcast about the habits of his elite players like LeBron, Rob said his top athletes would much rather do prehab than rehab.[10] Exactly. Early mornings have become a distinct advantage for me, but rest is even more significant to living in a way today that helps me thrive tomorrow.

A FOCUSED YOU

These strategies and others you develop will help produce a far less distracted you. A focused you is a better you.

Your attention is expensive. Every news organization and social media company knows that. Between carving out a quiet workspace to spend your Green Zone in, making the best of non-optimal conditions, silencing your devices, giving yourself space to think, and leveraging rest to fuel your energy, you're better positioned to spend your time on the things that you know have the most value to you.

But there's one more challenge and opportunity when it comes to realizing your priorities—people. It's hard to keep yourself focused, but when other people enter the picture, it gets even more complicated. That's why the next chapter is all about how to handle a priority hijacker that comes in the form of your fellow humans.

CHAPTER 8 IN A SNAP

- Average users touch their phones 2,617 times a day. Heavy users touch their phones 5,427 times a day.
- When technology runs us, it can ruin us. Technology makes a wonderful servant but a terrible master.
- ✔ If you're like most people, you don't need an enemy to interrupt you. You already have one: a perpetually distracted you.

- The opposite of distraction isn't focus; it's traction.

- Paying attention to the wrong things costs you your priorities. Your goals. Your productivity. Your health. Even your family. And eventually it costs you your potential and your dreams.

- In the same way that not all *hours* are created equal and not all *tasks* are created equal, not all *environments* are created equal.

- Find or create the most undistracted environment you can for your Green Zone.

- Notifications on your devices make you access content on other people's schedules, not yours.

- Most things that present themselves as urgent aren't urgent.

- The quality of your work is determined by the quality of your thinking.

- Early mornings can be especially productive, not because you don't notice the distractions but because those distractions aren't there in the first place.

- A focused you is a better you.

CHAPTER 9

WHAT ABOUT PEOPLE?

*What to Do When the Wrong People Want Your Attention
and the Right People Don't*

> Love is something more stern and splendid than
> mere kindness.
>
> —C. S. Lewis

Growing up, I spent a lot of time at my grandparents' house. Grandma was my main babysitter, a best friend, and someone who was like a second mother. Nobody could make homemade meatballs and fried chicken like hers, and there was always a bowl filled with M&M's in the living room. No wonder we kids loved being at her place so much.

Grandma also had a hard time figuring out how to handle one particular friend, whom I'll call Nancy. Nancy lived across town, but every morning at ten o'clock, she would call Grandma to talk. In those pre-cell-phone times, phones were big devices hung on the kitchen wall, with cords that stretched only so far.

If you were on the phone, you had about a five-foot radius of freedom in which you could travel before you either snapped the phone cord or pulled the base off the wall. So, most of the time, you either stood by the phone or pulled up a chair to talk.

My grandmother appreciated those conversations, but not nearly as much as Nancy seemed to. Grandma was ready for a fifteen-minute chat. Nancy, it seems, was ready for endless conversation every day. As the phone rang, I'd hear my grandmother say, "It's ten o'clock. That must be Nancy," and pick up the phone. They'd talk about a few things, but as is the case when you talk every day, there wasn't much news.

Then I'd watch Grandma try to unsnare herself from the conversation.

"That's so interesting, Nancy. It's been nice talking to you."

"Well, that's great to hear, Nancy. I suppose I have to make soup for lunch soon."

"Well, look at the time . . ."

Nancy never picked up on the clues. As in *never*. The fact that she had nothing to say didn't change the fact that she took all morning to say it.

Grandma would roll her eyes as Nancy talked on. Then she'd move her hand in a circular motion as if to say, "Wrap it up." She'd sit. Then she'd stand. Then she'd sigh.

My favorite was when, after an hour or so of Nancy, Grandma would enlist me. She'd cup her hand over the phone and, in a barely audible whisper, say to me, "Go outside and call me. Pretend like you need me."

So I'd head out the back kitchen door, through the porch, and down the stairs. Then I'd turn around, head back up the stairs and through the porch door, and yell, "Grandmaaaaaaa! Can you help me?"

And in her best surprised, staccato voice, Grandma would say, "Oh, Nancy, Carey needs me. Got to go. Bye."

And so ended the conversation.

I loved being her nuclear option.

My guess is you've probably got a Nancy or two in your life. Good people. Even good friends. But not exactly how you wanted to be spending your morning. Every morning.

THE PEOPLE PROBLEM

You've already realized that all the wrong things want your attention. And now you have strategies to combat that. But what about the most challenging interruption of all—people? What do you do with people like Nancy? People can be a wonderful investment for your Green Zone, but you also realize that sometimes people can completely waste it. Here's the truth: in the same way that all the wrong *things* want your attention, so do all the wrong *people*. Nothing against Nancy, but that's often the truth.

I realize it's not polite to say that and, because you're a civil person, part of you is pushing back right now, asking, "Wrong people? How can *people* be wrong? Doesn't *everyone* matter?"

Everybody does matter. But, you might admit, people tend to be the greatest opportunity and the greatest obstacle in your life. One CEO told me that allowing the wrong person into his Green Zone can reduce his peak energy from five hours to five minutes. When that bad meeting is over, the rest of the day becomes a Red Zone. Maybe you can relate.

So, our beautiful theory about a well-guarded Green Zone works perfectly until another human being gets between you and your priorities. And if you're like me—or my CEO friend who let

that one person onto his agenda against his better judgment—
you'll just cave. Or you'll become really insensitive to other people to try to block them out, and that always produces regret. The
Nancys of the world are wonderful people, and there are definitely times for them, but left unchecked, the Nancy moments
happen far too frequently for most of us.

YOU SHOULDN'T JUST DISTANCE YOURSELF

Humans have struggled with how to interact with one another
since we started populating the planet. It doesn't always go well.
According to the biblical book of Genesis, when there were
merely four people on Earth, the murder rate was 25 percent. For
millennia, people have relied on distance and differences between
people to desensitize them to one another.

Think about how you behave in a place as innocuous as the
grocery store. In the supermarket, as you're looking for frozen
cherries and oat milk, you're bolder and ruder when you have a
shopping cart in your hands than when you don't. Because your
cart also protects you as it rockets you forward, you can get to the
frozen food section faster than your aisle mate and more easily
than when it's just two lonely humans saying, "After you." "No,
after you."

Or think about how you conduct yourself in your car. Chances
are, you're naturally more aggressive there, too, occasionally cut-
ting people off, tailgating, honking your horn, and not caring
nearly as much as you normally do. Ask my wife how I behave on
a country road when somebody cuts me off and I'm in my 3,800-
pound SUV. I am incredibly brave . . . right up to the moment he
rolls down the window and invites me to pull over. Then I hit
Reverse and pretend not to speak English.

Remove the metal cages and stand face to face, and suddenly you're just human. It's hard to say no to people. Even if you think you should. Even if you're trying to protect the most valuable hours you have in a day. Distancing yourself from people or erecting hard barriers will diminish the quality of your life, not enrich it. It might be effective for getting people out of your personal space, but dehumanizing people and distancing yourself from them is hardly the recipe for a quality life.

So, what is? Let's probe a little further into the mystery of human interaction before we figure out how to handle the different kinds of people who want (or need) a slice of you.

SO WEIRD YET SO TRUE

Here's a paradox you might recognize: The people who want your time are rarely the people who should have your time. And the people who should get most of your premium time rarely ask you for it.

Keep that dynamic going, and the people who most drain you will be the people you spend most of your time with. And the people who most energize you? Yep, you'll spend the least amount of time with them.

Think about it. At work, your best team members, top salespeople, best managers, top donors, and best volunteers rarely if ever ask for your time. In your personal life, the people who often suffer most from your misallocation of time are the people closest to you—your spouse, kids, best friends, parents, and other family members. Too often you'll ignore the people you care about most as you spend your time with people you care about less.

If you recognize this dynamic (I do), then ask this question: *Why don't I spend time with the people I most want to and need to spend time with?*

Often you don't hang out with them because they're not particularly needy or demanding. The healthiest people rarely are. In addition, they don't cause problems, so you're not calling them in for a "talk." They're happily doing what they do well and generally don't ask you for your time.

The people who most want to meet with you are rarely the people you most need to meet with.

There are two categories of people you should be investing less time in (and almost no Green Zone time in). One is the people you feel you *should* meet with because, well, things aren't going well or they're in a crisis you feel needs your attention. The other is the people who want to meet with you but don't need to.

THE PEOPLE YOU FEEL YOU NEED TO MEET WITH (BUT DON'T WANT TO)

Think about the return on your time investment when you try to help the people you feel you should meet with (but don't necessarily want to). Often the common denominator is that they either are in crisis or are underperforming—the employee who's always late to work or the salesperson who isn't closing many deals or the accounts manager whose numbers never seem to add up or the friend who's always moving from bad relationship to bad relationship.

Your return on investment in this kind of encounter is usually quite low. Your motivational talk last month didn't make enough of a difference, so you take a harder line this month, hoping that helps. But—surprise, surprise—in all likelihood, you'll be back at it with this person again next month, still trying to figure out how to make it better. Despite your investment of time and energy, it never really gets better and there's always something new you need to address or respond to. Some people don't want to get better. They just want your time. Clinical psychologist John Townsend said people like this have "a flat learning curve."[1]

It's not that you should have zero time for people with flat learning curves, but they shouldn't take up your *prime* time when neither you nor they see any results. And even if they could use coaching or assistance, if your influence isn't helping them, maybe you're not the one to assist them. I've found more than a few times that the best thing I can do when I hit a flat-learning-curve dynamic in relationships is refer them to other people. It's not just better for me, but it's better for them.

This isn't just true at work; it can be true at home and in other areas of life. While family relationships are forever and friendships may last almost as long, there have been seasons in my parenting when it's become clear that I'm not the one who's going to coach my son through this moment. Instead, my wife's care and counsel have been far more what he needs. Other times that flips, and my sons have responded to me better. Same with friends. Healthy relationships are mutual. When mutuality or effectiveness in the relationship stops, it's time to reassess and recalibrate.

THE PEOPLE WHO WANT TO MEET WITH YOU
(BUT DON'T NEED TO)

In addition to people you feel you need to meet with, there are people who will want to meet with you. Some are great investments. We'll get to those soon. Some aren't—yet they'll ask for your time, take away nothing from the meeting, and leave you feeling drained. They want to meet with you but, honestly, don't need to because it won't be of much value to them or to you.

Here's a short (and incomplete) list of the kinds of people many of us find draining:

- drama queens or kings whose lives are a never-ending sea of turbulence
- perpetually angry or bitter people who are looking for a sounding board
- addicts who don't want help
- chronic complainers
- people who won't take responsibility for their lives or actions
- people who have a lot of time on their hands and no purpose or direction

The point here is *not* that we should avoid these people at all costs. Not at all. In fact, I think we should make room for some of them in our lives (some, after all, might be family). Everyone needs a hand, and in some seasons I've been the draining person who needed people to build into me. (On my bad days, I'm sure I'm probably still draining to some people around me.)

Social workers, counselors, health-care workers, mental health workers, pastors, and in varying degrees, first responders deal with needy people. These are all tremendous professions that provide vital services to people in need. In imbalanced relationships, you give; they receive. While that's appropriate in many cases, a steady diet of giving leaves you depleted.[2] It just becomes exhausting for you to have a *lot* of draining people in your life, and when they occupy your Green Zone regularly, you'll struggle to get anything done (as will they).

If you spend most of your time with draining people, you'll live much of your life feeling drained. So, guard your heart. While this might sound selfish, it's not. Self-care isn't selfish. It gives you (and me) the energy we need to truly be present for the people who may not be as energizing. You can give only what you've got. And if you've got nothing left in the tank, you can't help anybody. I meet so many leaders who have nothing left to give because they've given it all away to people who, honestly, weren't helped by the interaction.

So many leaders have nothing left to give because they've given it all away to people who, honestly, weren't helped by the interaction.

INVEST IN YOUR BEST

When I first understood that I would naturally spend most of my time with the people I least needed to and not nearly enough time with the people I most needed to, I experienced a breakthrough moment both in my life and in my leadership. Just because people wanted to meet with me didn't mean I needed to meet with them. So I took what I'd learned from the Pareto principle (described in chapter 7) and applied it to relationships.

Relationally speaking, the Pareto principle looks like this: spend most of your time with the people who produce most of your results and the least amount of time with the people who don't. In leadership, that typically means you should spend most of your time meeting with your top performers. In your personal life, spend 80 percent of your time with the people you care most about (family, close friends, mentors), leaving 20 percent for others.

There are some real benefits to spending 80 percent of your time on your inner circle. To begin with, your top and closest people will be thrilled you did. Second, *you'll* be energized when you spend time with them, as will they. Ditto with true friendship. It's mutual. And as you spend more time together, you'll develop deeper connections, overcome hurdles, and enjoy the life you've been given together.

Just as your meetings with non-performers were draining for both you and them, your meetings with your top people will be energizing for both of you. In addition, when you meet with your top people, they usually lean in even harder and produce better results. A further benefit is that investing time to keep your top people healthy and aligned has a trickle effect throughout your organization. Healthy at the top, healthy at the bottom. Unhealthy at the top, unhealthy at the bottom.

When you make these kinds of radical decisions and changes (if you take what I'm saying seriously, it *is* a radical change for most people), you end up with a lot more free time for people because you take all the time you used to spend on your low performers at work and spend it on your best people. And you take all the time you were spending on some of your not-really friends on social media and in your life and reinvest it in the people closest to you. That frees up not just time but mental energy. We spend a lot of time worrying about people and things we have no true influence over, and when you eliminate that worry from your life, the mental clarity and space you acquire is really quite astonishing. Plus, you'll have the time to grab lunch with your operations director who is crushing it, and enough energy left over to throw the ball in your backyard with your eight-year-old after dinner.

HOW MANY FRIENDS CAN ONE HUMAN BEING HAVE?

Figuring out the right and wrong people to keep meeting with is one thing, but it also prompts this fascinating question: Exactly how many relationships do you think one human being can have? British anthropologist and evolutionary psychologist Robin Dunbar said that the maximum number of meaningful personal relationships most humans can cultivate is much smaller than you might assume.

Dunbar argued that the number of relationships you can have is not just a matter of preference or willingness. He said that your limits are *cognitive*—they're hardwired. Dunbar's conclusion about the human capacity for relationships springs from the way the brain developed. Drawing from anthropology, biology, and human history dating back to ancient Greece and Rome, Dunbar broke down the limits of meaningful human relationships into a series of concentric circles.

Starting at the center circle, Dunbar suggested that you and I are hardwired for three to five true friendships—intimate relationships with people whom you have the habit of connecting with at least once a week. You don't even need to use your other hand to count the number of intimate friendships a human can have.

The next circle is the twelve to fifteen people he calls your "sympathy group"—friends you connect with at least once a month who share your values, interests, and often perspectives on life. "Curiously," he noted, "this is also the typical team size in most team sports, the number of members on a jury, the number of Apostles . . . and the list goes on." The total of twenty relationships between these first two circles is about all the people most humans can manage to truly know, said Dunbar.[3]

But wait . . . I know way more people than that, you're thinking. And you're right. You do "know" the names, bios, and perhaps the kids' names of a larger group. But Dunbar maxed that number out at 150. Not 300. Not 1,500. Not 1.5 million. Just 150.

Why that number? Dunbar noted that the average size of ancient and medieval villages was about 150 people. We were wired to live in meaningful communities of about that size. And somehow that number still plays out in the world today. The 150-person network corresponds to everything from the number of friends you send Christmas cards to (if you still send Christmas cards), to the need to abruptly shift management styles in an organization (150 or fewer employees can function as a single organism; beyond that, you have to create divisions and reorganize), to the size of companies in the military. Dunbar believed we have the bandwidth to meaningfully connect with this wider circle of 150 from time to time or at least once a year.[4]

When you think through how your life operates, you might find surprising resonance in what Dunbar observed. Chances are, your true inner circle isn't more than five. And you may well connect at least monthly with twelve to fifteen people who form the circle you call friends. And beyond that, there are probably about 150 people you connect with at parties, on vacations, at summer barbecues, at annual gatherings, or just by reaching out to stay in touch.

Dunbar's point is that these are fixed numbers. When someone new moves into your inmost circle of three to five, he said, someone has to drop out to make room for that person.[5] If you're not sure this actually happens, check how often you texted certain people over the last year and look at the last decade or two of pics you took on your birthday. Over time, close friendships come and go, but the number you can accommodate stays the same.

It appears that you and I are designed to process only a limited number of meaningful relationships. Which actually has some pretty staggering implications for how we live these days.

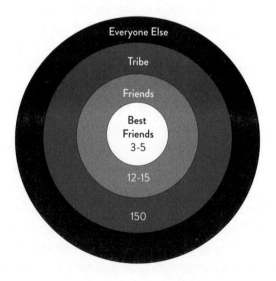

FRIENDS, FANS, AND FOLLOWERS

As Dunbar noted back in 2010, "It seems that the social networking sites have broken through the constraints of time and geography that limited people's social world" in the past.[6] If that was true in 2010, it's even more true today.

Even a quick check of your phone might show you that you have 754 friends on one social media channel, 192 followers on another, and 316 on a third—a historically unprecedented and rather unnatural number of people in your life.

The struggle, then, is between design and desire. You were *designed* to handle between three and 150 in a meaningful way, but being a social creature and not wanting to upset, anger, or disappoint people, your *desire* is to connect with far more.

When you give in to your desire to connect but don't think about design, you experience tension, because there's an implicit contract with many of the people we connect with on social media. Every time you share your phone number, give out your email address, or hit Accept, Follow, or Friend, it's like you make an unstated commitment—you're available and accessible. All the people you're now connected with have the ability to message you, tag you, or otherwise access you anytime, anywhere.

Do that more than 150 times (and I doubt there's a single reader of this book who's under 150), and you blow your natural limit. No wonder social media makes you feel overwhelmed. And you and I aren't exactly Justin Bieber.

Whether people connect with you to be nice, say hi, ask a question, respond to something you're doing, or ask whether you want to go for coffee or come over and watch the game Saturday night, you've got a decision on your hands. Do you click Like? Leave a comment? Answer their question? Hang out with them Saturday? Support their fundraiser?

Doing this for three to five people is sustainable, which is why the circle stays small. And when it stays small and the right people end up in your inner circle, it mostly feels natural, mutual, and life giving.

Being able to do this semiregularly for twelve to fifteen stretches you, but it works. Having some kind of connection with 150 probably pushes you to your limit.

But add the digital realm into the equation, and everything changes. Digital tries to expand you relationally beyond what you were designed to handle. While your relational network can keep growing, your capacity to connect with the people in it doesn't.

Add to that the reality that digital has a habit of showing up in the strangest and most intrusive ways. And when 450 or 4,500 people have access to you digitally, you get inundated in a way you can't possibly respond to without completely stressing yourself out.

People have far better manners than technology does. Face to face, most people see the nuance of whether it's a good time to ask someone a question or call in a favor. Generally speaking, we respect where our friends are at and err on the side of restraint rather than interruption.

Technology removes that nuance. Digital messages are always sent at the convenience of the sender, never at the convenience of the recipient. Digital proximity means anyone has access anytime, anywhere, which feels so overwhelming, especially when you're watching the sunset with the people you love most. Physical proximity has good manners that digital proximity hasn't learned.

HEY, BUDDY

A final unusual element of the digital world is that digital proximity not only gives us disproportionate access to people at strange moments but in addition creates unnatural relationships. I'm not talking about nurturing an inappropriate chat with the man or woman you had a crush on in high school. I'm talking about how technology bends the way we relate to people.

Next time you're sorting through your messages or social feed, do a quick audit of how many times someone says "Love you" or "Hey, buddy" or "BFFs forever" or some other expression of affection. Then ask yourself, *Is this the kind of relationship I'm really capable of having with all these people?*

I'm not trying to be a killjoy here or argue that you should give everyone you know a dispassionate handshake, but here are two questions. First, can your emotional capacity expand enough to cover all these new relationships? Second, are the people who are telling you how much they love you part of your five, your fifteen, or even your 150?

The deepest relationships rightly belong with the closest connections. I'm not arguing that there isn't something to love in everyone. There is. You simply can't be close enough to most people to have an authentic, deep, mutual relationship with them. Yet the language we're all increasingly using has lost sight of that.

Every one of those digital access points involves some kind of *commitment.*

As a result, you lose your own priorities in the process of promising too much to too many, only to end up with too little to share—too little time, too little energy, and too little bandwidth to say yes to everything that comes your way, but you say yes anyway. The number of digital requests is far bigger than the number you were designed to handle.

What should you do with all this?

I suggest using Dunbar's numbers as your digital filter. Identify the three to five in your inner circle and the twelve to fifteen in your support group. And while you likely don't need to name the wider 150, keep that concept in mind when you get a request, and ask yourself, *Is this person someone I'm in a real relationship with?*

Then respond accordingly.

Get back to your three to five as quickly as you can, because they are your lifeblood. Go to their games. Grab dinner. Support their fundraisers. Hang out and watch the sunset.

Reply to your next twelve to fifteen with a little less urgency, but treat them like they matter to you, because they do.

The 150 are people you want to value and appreciate, but you don't need to give them the kind of immediate response you'd give to the innermost circles. And the rest of humanity? Well, be kind, but put up some boundaries. You literally weren't designed to handle that many people.

I've found this strategy to be helpful. The online content I produce gets accessed over 1.5 million times a month, so I get a *lot* of messages. I have a team that processes much of it, but I'm still engaged. I'll spend ten to thirty minutes a day responding personally. My team does the rest, and then I'm free to be with my three to five and twelve to fifteen and occasionally with my 150. And, for the most part, I keep my sanity.

If you're going to reduce your stress and increase your joy, focusing on those smaller circles is key.

So, let's get really specific.

Who are your best friends, your three to five?

Who are your twelve to fifteen?

For your tribe, no need to list a full 150 names unless you really want to, but the idea here is these are people you need to get back to and keep in contact with, but they're not your best friends or the twelve to fifteen friends you're tracking with regularly.

And everyone else? Well, all you need to know is they're not your best friends, friends, or really part of your tribe.

Now, here's the next step.

Decide how quickly you'll respond to and how often you'll reach out to your best friends, friends, and tribe. The principle is simple: stop treating everyone the same, because all relationships aren't the same. The depth of the relationship should determine the depth and speed of your response.

I respond to my family pretty much immediately, and my phone is programmed to let them ring through no matter where I am or what I'm doing. I also happen to have one wife and two kids, so it's a pretty tiny circle. And my family doesn't ping me every thirty seconds, so that works just fine.

But on to friends. I'll get back to my three to five within the hour, unless I'm in the middle of really deep work in my Green Zone.

I usually get back to my twelve to fifteen within a few hours and always within the same day.

My tribe? Probably same day or within forty-eight hours, depending on how they're trying to reach me.

Everyone else? Those are people I or my team will get back to within a few days or sometimes not at all. You simply place these people on a task list and get back to them in your normal workflow down the road. The depth of your response should be gauged by the depth of the relationship. Unless you really want to connect deeply with that person you met at the conference last summer in San Diego, you really don't need to drop what you're doing to compose a long, thoughtful response.

This approach solves an age-old problem—that the people

you care about least end up taking up the time you should be spending on the people you care about most. The people who need you most should get an undistracted you. Others can wait.

The depth of the relationship should determine the depth and speed of your response.

PLEASING THE RIGHT PEOPLE

Deep down, most of us are people pleasers. I am. The challenge with people-pleasing, of course, is that you end up pleasing all the wrong people and ignoring the right ones. I hope this has helped you sort through the maze of relationships that make up life today. The filters and criteria you've learned should help you do the things that matter most with the people who matter most and be surprisingly undistracted doing so.

When you do that well, your Green Zone will produce far more than you imagined it could, and your Yellow and Red Zones can absorb the necessary relationships that are left. The rest? Well, your filters are strong enough now to simply let some of them go. You know what matters most and who matters most, and you're ready to rebuild your life.

Speaking of life, though, before we wrap up, we'll turn to one more strategy that will help you realize this theory in real life. It involves your calendar. This will help you cement all the progress you've made and make it part of your daily reality. Ready?

CHAPTER 9 IN A SNAP

- People tend to be the greatest opportunity and the greatest obstacle.
- The people who want your time are rarely the people who should have your time. And the people who *should* get most of your premium time rarely ask you for it.
- Healthy relationships are mutual.
- If you spend most of your time with draining people, you'll live much of your life feeling drained.
- Spend most of your time with the people who produce most of your results and the least amount of time with the people who don't. In your personal life, spend 80 percent of your time with the people you care most about, leaving 20 percent for others.
- The number of relationships people can have is not just a matter of preference or willingness; the limits are cognitive, having to do with the way the brain works.
- People are hardwired for three to five close friendships, twelve to fifteen friendships, and 150 personal relationships.
- You were designed to handle between three and 150 relationships in a meaningful way, but social media will pressure you to connect with far more.
- Despite being designed to handle up to 150 personal relationships, social media pressures you to connect with far more people.
- People have far better manners than technology does.

- Messages are always sent at the convenience of the sender, never at the convenience of the recipient.

- The deepest relationships rightly belong with the closest connections.

- Stop treating everyone the same, because all relationships aren't the same. The depth of the relationship should determine the depth and speed of your response.

PART 5

THEORY, MEET REAL LIFE

THE BIG SYNC

*How to Synchronize Your Time, Energy, and
Priorities Every Day*

> You don't think your way into a new kind of living
> but live your way into a new kind of thinking.
>
> —Henri Nouwen

If you reflect on how your time gets spoken for, you'll be amazed at how often it happens because you get caught off guard.

When my kids were still in elementary school, I walked into a Tuesday night board meeting. Jason pulled me aside.

"What are you doing next Saturday?" he asked.

I pulled out my calendar, looked at Saturday, and saw it was empty. "Um, nothing," I replied with a half smile. Inside, I was wincing.

"What are you doing next Saturday?" is rarely an innocent question. It usually means "I have an idea that involves something you don't want to do . . . like helping me move a piano."

My mind started racing as I saw the problem I was getting myself into. Jason was a great guy, but he was not really a close friend. He wasn't even one of my 150. What did he want with my Saturday?

Saturday was *supposed* to be my day off. It was the only day that week when the boys and Toni were home at the same time, and I had promised I'd be with them. I wasn't working. No school. No work. Just us.

Why don't I tell him that?

Why can't I tell him that?

What's he going to say next?

I thought about what Toni would say when I got home. That conversation would not go well at all.

I could already hear her saying, "How could you say yes on your only day off? Why didn't you ask me? How come you said yes to him and no to your kids? Honestly, Carey. Really?"

And, of course, she would be right. One hundred percent right.

Jason snapped me back to the moment.

"Great!" he said. "We're having a party at my place Saturday afternoon with a bunch of people from my work. Want to come? I'd love for you to meet them."

Well, now I felt trapped. What could I say? *I don't want to go to your party.* (Making me a complete social failure and jerk.) *Hey, Jason, that's supposed to be my day off.* (Well, that's awkward.) *Let me check with Toni.* (I'd be throwing her under the bus. Man . . .).

I resurrected my half smile, put on a well-mannered voice, and eked out, "Uh, sure, I'd love to go."

There it was—*another* Saturday when I was not doing what I really wanted or needed to do.

And that's the problem with blank space on your calendar. Again and again, it trips you up.

BLANK SPACE IS A TRAP

Blank space on your calendar is a trap. It looks like freedom, but it's really jail disguised as liberty. The moment you think the white space on your calendar gives you freedom, disappointment is right around the corner.

For all the reasons we've covered so far, there are a thousand things that will command your attention on any day that looks free and clear on your calendar. The most important things will get hijacked by urgent things you never planned on doing. You'll be disappointed, and the people closest to you will pay a price.

> *Blank space on your calendar is a trap. It looks like freedom, but it's really jail disguised as liberty.*

What you'll discover, though, is that the key to helping you thrive is to schedule all your priorities (including family time). Moving to a fixed calendar—which we'll call the Thrive Calendar—ties together everything we've learned so far and makes it work in your everyday life. Developing your own Thrive Calendar will protect your Green Zone, leverage your Yellow and Red Zones, and ensure that the things and people that matter to you are the things you spend your time on.

It's also the opposite of how I used to live and how most people live.

To demonstrate that, take a moment and pull out your calendar right now, whether that's on your phone, on your laptop, or an old-school paper calendar.

I'm serious—do that. I'll wait.

Got it?

Flip ahead six months from today's date.

What do you see?

Most people would see not much, if anything.

Maybe you have a dentist appointment or a vacation or a family function you've booked for the third Friday of the month. But if you're like the vast majority of people, chances are you see *nothing*. Your calendar is blank.

And that's the problem.

Blank calendars create all kinds of issues. On the one hand, they engender a deep and pervasive false hope. You think about how busy you are right now, but you look ahead to six months from now or even two weeks from now, see all the blank space, and think that relief is coming.

Only that's what you thought six months ago—and again last week—when you looked at your calendar, and just the opposite happened.

Despite all the blank space, you get slammed, again and again.

CONTROL YOUR CALENDAR SO OTHERS STOP CONTROLLING YOU

A blank calendar is pretty much a guarantee that you'll spend your time on everyone else's priorities, not yours. There are more than a few Jasons in your life (well meaning as they are) who are always asking you what you're up to, and as soon as you say "Not much," you're at a party you weren't planning to attend, playing golf when you really wanted to watch movies with your kids, or helping somebody move.

To change that, decide how you'll spend your time before others decide for you. If you don't decide ahead of time how to spend your time, others will, which is a ticket both to feeling overwhelmed and to ensuring you accomplish nothing that's important to you. Instead, decide in advance what you're going to do, and put it on your calendar. Not only does that make the art of saying no that much easier, but it also makes it dignified and almost automatic.

Decide how you'll spend your time before others decide for you.

Prescheduling your calendar is different from keeping a to-do list. So many overwhelmed people have long to-do lists but get no further ahead. In fact, they just fall further behind. The reason they fail at task management is that they have a clear sense of *what* matters but not a clear sense of *when* to get it done. Taking charge of your calendar puts you in control of your day, not your day in control of you. Your intentions become your new rhythm. Scheduling what matters most is how you ensure you do what you're best at when you're at your best and stay in the Thrive Cycle. Calendaring your Green, Red, and Yellow Zones and scheduling your priorities is the final strategic move you need to make to turn what you've learned into the reality you live.

THE THRIVE CALENDAR

Underneath the Thrive Calendar is a simple concept. A fixed calendar is a predecision about how to spend your work and personal time, most often in repeating appointments with yourself, week after week, year after year.

Embracing the Thrive Calendar means you'll schedule time (ahead of time) to

- do what you're best at when you're at your best
- develop your gift
- work on your business, not just in your business
- rest
- connect with family
- nurture your spiritual life
- spend most of your people time with your best people
- do your least energizing work when you're least energetic

Best of all, it's simple. Because you're going to set up *repeating* appointments with yourself (for example, "Strategic planning every day from 7 to 9 a.m." or "Coffee with Jeff on the third Thursday of every month at 10 a.m."), this doesn't take you two hours a week to set up. In fact, it takes you no time most weeks because you've set the patterns in advance. Once you set it up, you forget it until you need to recalibrate, which might be every year or every few months in seasons of rapid change. Otherwise, it just runs in the background while your life runs much better. It's effective because you've scheduled the things and people nobody ever asks you to schedule—your priorities that always seem to get hijacked.

Because content creation is some of the most valuable work I do, I devote much of my Green Zone each day to it. I don't need to get more specific than that on my calendar, because I'm always writing something. I just set aside the time to write, and every day I work on something from my task list during those hours.

Although he never talked about a Green Zone or a Thrive Cycle, Ernest Hemingway adopted a similar discipline, usually sitting down at dawn most mornings to write. As Hemingway told George Plimpton in a 1958 interview for the *Paris Review*:

> When I am working on a book or a story I write every morning as soon after first light as possible. There is no one to disturb you and it is cool or cold and you come to your work and warm as you write. . . . You write until you come to a place where you still have your juice and know what will happen next and you stop and try to live through until the next day when you hit it again. You have started at six in the morning, say, and may go on until noon or be through before that.[1]

Talk about using your prime hours to develop your gift.

The point is simple: you become what you repeatedly do. When you co-opt the rhythms of your everyday life to work for you, not against you, it changes everything.

Everyone's calendar looks different, but before you set up yours, I'll share a few examples of priorities I fix in my Thrive Calendar:

- I spend my first hour every day quietly, sipping hot tea, reflecting, praying, and reading Scripture. For me, that's the building block of my life, so I write it into my calendar.
- I save my mornings for things that I'm best at and that energize me—writing, thinking, strategizing, planning. But mostly writing.
- I block off some evenings and weekends for personal and family time.

- I keep Fridays free of scheduled meetings so I can finish projects, dream a little, do some errands, and on good weeks, take off early.
- Meetings usually have to fit into designated slots in the afternoon or late morning once I'm out of my Green Zone. I set a maximum number of meetings every week (these days, it's fifteen). Exceptions have to be just that— exceptions for critical reasons.

Again, your calendar *will* look different and should look different from mine. You need to tailor it to your gifting, calling, and circumstances.

DESIGNING YOUR THRIVE CALENDAR

By setting aside a few hours every day to tackle whatever matters most to you professionally and personally, you'll be able to experience the kind of productivity and nurtured relationships that you thought was impossible. Maximizing your Yellow and Red Zones produces similar results.

There are four key decisions for you to make when you design your Thrive Calendar:

1. Decide *what* you will and won't do within each zone.
2. Decide *whom* you will and won't meet with.
3. Decide *when* you'll do specific tasks within each zone.
4. Decide *where* you'll do your work, especially your Green Zone work.

Your Green Zone is, of course, the most important zone to protect in your Thrive Calendar. If you craft your Green Zone well, your Yellow and Red Zones can act as catch basins for some of the daily issues that crop up, as well as for your regular work that doesn't rank high enough for Green Zone space. And having worked through the concepts in the book, you hopefully have a much better filter by now for leaving numerous things off the calendar altogether.

Step 1: Revisit Your Energy Clock

In chapter 4, you put together your personal Energy Clock. If a bit of time has passed, this is a good opportunity to revisit it. It's time to integrate your clock even more with your daily rhythms and routines.

Here, again, for illustration purposes, is mine:

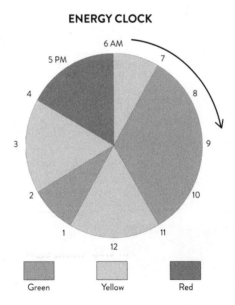

ENERGY CLOCK

Step 2: Sync Your Zones with Your Priorities

It's now time to sync your zones with your most important priorities—both tasks and people. Using what you learned in chapter 6 when you first outlined your priorities and what you ~~picked up in chapter 9 about people, fill out~~ the chart below. Keep the priorities at the broadest level. If planning is part of your job, just keep it as "planning" rather than "plan fourth-quarter off-site," which belongs on a task list. You want to calendar only your appropriate priorities in each zone.

You can see how I've zoned my various priorities and people here. A good rule for people is your top three to five get into your Green Zone if you're using your Green Zone to meet with people—or perhaps your top twelve to fifteen on an occasional basis. Or, of course, you can use your Green Zone mostly for tasks. It all depends on what you want to accomplish. Mine looks like this.

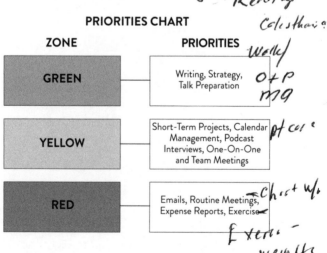

PRIORITIES CHART

ZONE	PRIORITIES
GREEN	Writing, Strategy, Talk Preparation
YELLOW	Short-Term Projects, Calendar Management, Podcast Interviews, One-On-One and Team Meetings
RED	Emails, Routine Meetings, Expense Reports, Exercise

▼ Download your Priorities Chart template at www.AtYourBestToday.com

Step 3: Schedule Time to Do What You're Best at When You're at Your Best

Finally, to truly be at your best, block time to do what you're best at when you're at your best by assigning priorities to your Green, Yellow, and Red Zones.

What you most want to establish in your calendar is your ongoing patterns for each zone. Your calendar will reflect the Task Chart priorities you've just outlined and will set them up in repeating appointments so you ensure you not only do what you're best at when you're at your best but also make ample space for your most critical tasks and relationships. And remember, when designing your calendar, think about your life, not just your leadership. Don't overcrowd it, and budget time for rest, because you bring you wherever you go. A rested you is a better you, so think holistically when you design your zones and patterns.

In the sample calendar below, which is based on my current patterns, you can see that the zones are all protected and general priorities have slots. You can add specific tasks and appointments (coffee with Devon at 3:00 p.m. on Monday or project briefing with team at 4:00 p.m. on Thursday) on top of this, but the rhythms should be the same week to week. As you already know, your life and mine consist of a series of ongoing patterns, so you should build the healthiest ones into your weekly schedule ahead of time. And if you want to extend the calendar into the evening hours, do so. Just write things such as "personal time," "family," "date night," "movie night" or whatever you want to do to ensure you don't end up working until 10:00 p.m. every night and to have a clear sense of how you'll spend those evening hours. This can be a fantastic strategy to guard against spending most nights toggling between Netflix and your email inbox when you owe it to yourself and the people you love to be off.

THRIVE CALENDAR

	SUNDAY	MONDAY	TUESDAY	WEDNESDAY	THURSDAY	FRIDAY	SATURDAY
6:00AM – 7:00AM	108	Personal Time	Personal Time	Personal Time	Personal Time	Personal Time *It·my Sa*	*CONT*
8:00AM							
9:00AM – 10:00AM	Family and Personal Time	Writing	Strategy	Talk Preparation	Strategy	Writing	Family and Personal Time
11:00AM							
12:00PM – 1:00PM		Short-Term Projects + Lunch	Calendar Management + Lunch	Meeting + Lunch	Meeting + Lunch	Strategy + Lunch	
2:00PM		Podcast Prep	Writing	Strategy	Writing	Projects	
3:00PM – 4:00PM		Podcast Interviews	Meetings + Admin	Podcast Interviews	Meetings + Admin	Planning + Admin	
5:00PM – 6:00PM		Exercise + Free Time	Meetings + Free Time	Exercise + Free Time	Admin + Free Time	Exercise + Free Time	

Green   Yellow   Red

Now, a reality check. Will my week or your week ever turn out like that in real life? Not always. Life happens. Meetings pop up, work piles up, and the kids have commitments, but now you can see what you are committed to doing. But if you guarded your Green Zone most days (or every day), then your most important objectives are done. And you would have also protected your rest and family times.

Adding your specific meetings to the base Thrive Calendar also gives you an idea of how busy your week is in advance. Remember, once you set up your Thrive Calendar, you can look ahead six months from now and have an idea of what that month and those weeks are going to be like and make choices accordingly.

Because you are planning ahead and can see your schedule well in advance, you'll know that you're on the road for ten days in October and much of that Green Zone time will be spent in airports, on flights, in hotels, and at events. Knowing that, you can reduce the number of meetings you have the week before and week after to make sure your Green Zone is especially protected. No more surprises.

So, go ahead and take your first run at your personal Thrive Calendar. This is how you move everything you've learned from theory to reality, from your imagination to your life.

You're deciding how you'll spend your time before others decide for you. And that's the key to thriving.

▼ Download your Thrive Calendar template at
www.AtYourBestToday.com

WAIT ... WHAT ABOUT MY TEAM?

You're probably thinking this might be a really great design for solopreneurs and executives who have full control of their calendars. But what about teams? What happens if you're not in control of your calendar and your boss tells you that you have to be at a meeting right in the heart of your Green Zone?

This might be a good time to recall—as we covered earlier—that as much as you *feel* you have no control, you likely have remarkable control over 128 to 148 of your 168 hours each week. Most workweeks are about 40 hours, and rarely in a knowledge-worker environment does your employer dictate how you spend 100 percent of your working hours. Even if he or she does, you get to do what you want with 128.

But back to the team question. What happens if, say, your

leadership team of five has two early risers who have morning Green Zones, two night owls whose Green Zones are later afternoon, and one person somewhere in between?

The best strategy is for all of you to quit and start your own organizations.

Kidding.

This is where team discussions come in really handy. One large organization I worked with in Atlanta mapped out their teams' zones on a flowchart, only to discover that their weekly executive team meeting was scheduled during everyone's Red Zone. When they saw this, they literally laughed out loud. Suddenly it became clear why no one liked that meeting, why they never seemed to get anything done, and why everyone wished it were shorter. They moved the meeting to a time when the team members were either in Green or in Yellow Zone territory, and things improved dramatically.

Maybe the reason everyone hates the Friday afternoon meeting is not that it's Friday afternoon but that most people are trying to stay awake.

Finding team rhythms is a question of compromise. Some meetings or activities might warrant taking up a lot of Green Zone bandwidth among team members. Others might fit better into most people's Yellow Zones (that's where I hold many of mine). And quick routine meetings might work in a Red Zone if they're not critical. And even in those moments when you have to gather and most team members are in their Red Zones, simply acknowledging that and moving through things as expeditiously as possible can feel like a gift.

When it comes to managing a team's time and energy, greater awareness is the first step toward greater effectiveness.

A MUCH BETTER RESPONSE TO JASON

Now, back to Jason, who wasn't trying to hijack my priorities. He was just trying to advance his.

If I'd had a Thrive Calendar back then and Jason had asked me what I was doing next Saturday, it would have been a very different conversation.

I would have taken out my calendar, looked at Saturday, looked Jason in the eye, and said, "Oh, I have a commitment."

Guess what Jason probably would have said? "Oh, that's too bad. I have a party at my place, and I would have loved for you to be there."

And I would have replied, "Thanks, Jason. I appreciate it. It was kind of you to think of me."

Ninety-nine percent of the time, that would end the conversation.

You don't need to tell Jason that the commitment is to yourself or your kids or your spouse. You simply have a commitment.

Healthy people respect the boundaries you set. Despite your lingering apprehension, the vast majority of the time, people won't question what that commitment is. They'll simply say, "Oh, that's too bad."

If they ask what you have going on, just tell them, "I have a commitment with my family that day." Or "I have some personal plans on Saturday." They'll get it. And respect it.

If you're still not sure that will work, you're probably worried about the tiny percentage of the population that's unhealthy. Unhealthy people will say things like "Can't you take your day off some other time?" Or "Does your family mean more to you than I do?"

The correct answers to those questions, respectively, are no and yes.

Is it awkward? Sure.

Is it better to protect the people and things that matter most? You bet it is.

I'm getting better at living through those awkward moments. I used to feel guilty and cave in. I don't anymore. You don't owe them an explanation beyond your no except a polite "Well, I'm sorry I won't be able to help you, but thanks for asking." Then shift the conversation to a new topic, or if they won't stop, close the conversation and politely walk away. Other people's needs don't have to become your guilt.

SIGNS THE THRIVE CYCLE IS WORKING

The Thrive Cycle is designed to be a virtuous loop. While the Stress Spiral pulls you down, the Thrive Cycle moves you into a much more sustainable pace.

Often when I read a book like this or take a course and try to implement the strategies I've just learned, I have a nagging question: How do I know I'm doing this right? It's like being at the gym. You think you've mastered squats until a trainer comes along, adjusts your stance, and tells you to do it again. Quivering and wincing, you go down again, saying to yourself, *So, that's a squat.*

The Thrive Cycle should leave you feeling totally different from how you would feel during that workout. Your life and leadership should feel *easier*, not harder. Sure, you're making some tough calls (like saying no), but when the Thrive Cycle is working, you should see these markers:

1. *You're accomplishing your priorities.* You're tackling your most important priorities because you scheduled them in advance, and you're doing them when you're at your best.
2. *You're getting better at what you do.* Because you're develop-

ing your gift, not just using it, you're seeing increasing returns on your investment of time in both your key tasks
and your key relationships. Give yourself a few months for
this one, but once you start getting some development
reps in, you'll feel a little like Hemingway: the more you
do it, the easier it gets.

3. *You love meeting with people again.* We've talked a lot about
   the challenges of meeting with people, but here's what's
   fun when the strategy is working: you'll *love* meeting with
   people again. Because you've prioritized whom you need
   to meet with, meetings are mostly energizing. Everyone's
   in the right place, and you've allotted each person the
   right time.

4. *You have time for yourself and your family.* You're no longer
   giving the things that matter most your leftover time and
   energy. Your family is getting some Green Zone time on
   your days off, and you're going home on weekdays with energy left in the tank rather than feeling completely drained.

5. *You're happier.* Because the big things that matter most are
   done, you feel significantly more relaxed. You're stressing
   less, and while life is still challenging at times, you feel a
   growing happiness you didn't have before or lost somewhere along the way.

Naturally, your day-to-day will vary, but if you're not feeling
most of those five markers most of the time, then take another
look at your Thrive Cycle rhythms. Maybe your Energy Clock
needs some adjustment, or you've got to play with how you're
spending your Green, Red, and Yellow Zones. Or perhaps your
calendar looks right but you're not living it. You've worked
through too many Saturdays when your calendar says "Family
Time." Or you're cheating sleep or your workouts.

I've adjusted my Thrive Calendar dozens of times over the years because life keeps changing.

In the next chapter, I'll give you some strategies to do that. Because, I promise you, you'll get into an optimal rhythm and be five for five in the list I just gave . . . and then the unpredictability of life will try to suck you right back into the Stress Spiral. You'll learn how to make sure that doesn't happen and that everything you've learned so far really does set you up to thrive for years to come.

CHAPTER 10 IN A SNAP

- Blank space on your calendar is a trap. It looks like freedom, but it's really jail disguised as liberty.

- The key to helping you thrive is to schedule all your priorities ahead of time.

- Decide how you'll spend your time before others decide for you. A blank calendar is pretty much a guarantee that you'll spend your time on everyone else's priorities, not yours.

- Prescheduling your calendar is different from keeping a to-do list. So many overwhelmed people have long to-do lists but get no further ahead. In fact, they just fall further behind.

- A fixed calendar is a predecision about how to spend your work and personal time, most often in repeating appointments with yourself, week after week, year after year.

- You become what you repeatedly do.

- When it comes to managing a team's time and energy, greater awareness is the first step toward greater effectiveness.

- Healthy people respect the boundaries you set. Unhealthy people don't.

THRIVE ON

*How to Recalibrate When Life Blows Up Your
Perfectly Crafted Plan*

No battle plan survives contact with the enemy.

—Military Axiom

We've been all the way through the Thrive Cycle and put it to
work for you with the Thrive Calendar. You might think we've
escaped the sucking vortex of the Stress Spiral and left stress far
behind.

Ha ha. If only.

Stress is so pervasive that it can pull you back in a heartbeat.
The pro tips and strategies I've shared so far are there for a reason: overwhelm, overcommitment, and overwork knock on my
door every day, as they will yours. Worse, stress is highly skilled at
home invasions. The strategies you've learned will keep stress off
your property unless you let your guard down. Or sometimes
stress gets in because your circumstances have changed enough

that your Thrive Calendar and the way you're approaching time, energy, and priorities need rebooting. That's what this chapter is designed to do—to give you expert-level skills for recalibrating when life blows up your perfectly crafted plan so you can get back to living in a way today that will help you thrive tomorrow.

I've stayed out of burnout for a decade and a half not just because of what you've learned so far but also because of what you're about to read next. Life is difficult and complicated. And when stress seeps back in, the adjustment strategies you'll find in this chapter should get you back on track almost immediately. Acting quickly and recalibrating fast are pretty intuitive. But when you get to what I call "do the math," you might think you clicked on some weird movie for nerds only. Hang in there. The strange percentages of time with people versus time alone, time you spend in meetings, and time you spend on the road have paid huge dividends in my life and the lives of others. It's often these unseen factors that undermine your well-being, and until you can name them, you have no idea why life and leadership aren't fun anymore.

A SEXY, TOXIC RELATIONSHIP

Before we dive into the strategies that will help you stay on track or get back on track, a final thought about stress. One of the reasons stress is so pervasive is that, in the strangest way, it is kind of attractive. As much as you might think you hate being stressed, stress has become such a universal condition that it's almost *sexy*.

You ready for this? There's a part of you that likes being stressed. Your friends enjoy it a bit too much as well. In this culture, you almost *have* to be stressed. For an ambitious person, it's rather unthinkable not to be stressed. When you start to live the

Thrive Cycle and you find yourself loving your Green Zone, you might think there's something wrong because you're having too much fun and getting far too many things done.

Because you're not nearly as stressed, you'll wonder whether you're not living up to your potential. What if you're slacking? Failing? Maybe you're even lazy? You've lived stressed so long you don't remember what unstressed feels like.

If you had to be dead honest with yourself, you sheepishly feel like you *need* stress. You, uh, *like* stress. It's validating. Am I right?

Stress is a good bad word. Our culture hates stress yet thrives on it. As a result, the pullback toward stress is almost gravitational. Stress is a badge of honor in the hamster-wheel life everybody's living.

If you're going to live in the Thrive Cycle long term, the best thing you can do is break up with stress and decide once and for all you're just not going to live that way. Stress will keep texting you, making false promises, and swearing that this time it will be better. Regardless, the smart thing is to walk away. It's a toxic relationship.

Stress is a good bad word. Our culture hates stress yet thrives on it.

HEY, LIFE, YOU'RE RUINING MY FLOW HERE

You may soon get to a place where the Thrive Cycle is working far better than you imagined it would. You're doing things and spending time with people you felt you never had time for before. You're back at the gym. You're sleeping well at night. You have more family time than you've had in years. And you're crushing the projects at work.

You're in the flow. You feel like you have more time for what matters most, because you do. You may be afraid to say it out loud, but it almost feels like you're thriving.

But it will all come crashing down way sooner than you think, unless you decide it won't. The good news is there are often warning signs that your current flow is about to be threatened. Here's a list of some of the things that will throw off your beautifully designed calendar and make your Thrive Cycle rhythms wobble:

- growth
- a promotion
- a new job
- having a child
- staff hires
- staff departures
- travel
- moving
- a change in your health
- the loss of a loved one
- a personal crisis
- a breakup
- a crisis in the life of someone close to you
- losing a job
- decline or malaise in your company or industry
- a new hobby
- new friends
- vacation

What do you do when life inevitably interrupts your well-designed plans? You can't hire or hope your way out of overwhelm. Instead, you need to lead yourself out of it.

Most people change when the pain associated with the status quo is greater than the pain associated with change. They spend months (or years) letting circumstances determine their stress levels and happiness levels.

Wise people don't wait to adapt. If you can see overwhelm coming, if you feel it tapping at your door, get proactive. Don't wait to go under before you recalibrate.

Your life and leadership are constantly changing, and your approach needs to change with them. In an overwhelmed culture, your agility is the cap on your ability.

Here are some practices that will help you keep thriving despite changing conditions. Once you understand them, it's not that difficult to adapt quickly and effectively.

In an overwhelmed culture, your agility is the cap on your ability.

ACT AS SOON AS YOU ANTICIPATE

Some change comes at you from out of the blue, but much of it doesn't. At times, you get a warning when your world is about to be altered. In the same way new parents get a nine-month warning that life is about to change forever, sometimes your boss gives you a heads-up that your promotion takes effect in a month, or you know you have two weeks until your new location opens, a year until you move, or a few weeks until you head to the beach for a break. You actually do get a heads-up on a lot of change you'll encounter.

When you get even a bit of advance notice, one of the best things you can do is start planning at once. Take some time to anticipate how your rhythms might change. Maybe right now you love 5:00 to 8:00 a.m. as your most productive time. Chances are, your new daughter is not going to value your morning sanctuary the way you do, at least in the first few months. Do you need to cut your expectations back to one hour of productive time in the morning for a few months (or none if you're the stay-at-home parent)?

If you've got new staff coming on board, can you do the pending reorganization now, checking in with the team and helping them adjust to the inevitable change? Adding new staff is a chance to look at how you spend your time too. Maybe you'll have too many direct reports once the new hire arrives, and you can do the reporting shuffle in advance.

If you anticipate the systemic change you'll need to make, you'll be far better off than if you just let the change happen and respond after or if you don't respond at all and wonder where your peace of mind went. I know this may sound elemental, but so few people make anticipatory changes. Waiting until it happens often means forfeiting your peace and your productivity.

You may not anticipate perfectly what the change is going to feel like, and that's normal. So as it happens and after it happens, tweak things again. Move another meeting. Shift your day. Get up earlier. Or get up later. Do what you need to do to thrive.

Fixing things before they break is a little like doing preventive maintenance on a car.

A few years ago, I bought a used SUV and racked up three hundred thousand miles on it before I traded it in for something new. Being a neat freak, I waxed it every year and kept the interior looking new, but the real story was that people kept asking me how I got so many miles out of it.

What's the secret to keeping a vehicle on the road that long? As much as I threw my elbow grease into the wax job, it wasn't a shiny exterior that kept it running. It's simple. Preventive maintenance. I did every recommended service when it was due or before it was due. Which meant I replaced the air filter before the air filter got clogged. Changed the transmission fluid before the transmission started slipping gears. Changed the oil at or before the recommended interval.

Fixing something before it breaks is far less costly than fixing it after it breaks, in terms of both time and money. I got the few hundred dollars I spent every year in preventive maintenance back multiple times over by being able to drive a reliable SUV for years after others had consigned theirs to the junkyard.

Preventive maintenance on your life works the same way. If you anticipate, instigate. Doing something before change happens is the best way to be ready when change happens. And if you need to tweak or reboot again after the change, no problem.

This can sound very theoretical, so let's get practical. When you see or sense change happening, here are five questions that can help you act as you anticipate:

1. *What's about to change?*
2. *What opportunities and obstacles will the change likely present?*
3. *What's most likely to happen to the demands on my time?*
4. *What's most likely to happen to my energy levels? (Note: Any*

change that involves loss or triggers sadness will likely reduce your energy levels at least temporarily. The greater the loss, the greater the loss of energy.)

5. *What adjustments can I make to my Thrive Calendar now to prepare for the new reality?*

RECALIBRATE ... FAST

Sometimes you can see change coming, but often you can't—you won't be able to see the problem until things break down. When that happens, and it will occur often, come back to some of the fundamentals of the Thrive Cycle and prepare to recalibrate your Thrive Calendar.

One of the best ways to begin this process is by tracking how you've *actually* been spending your time recently. Even though you're far more conscious of how you're spending your time now than you were before you embraced the Thrive Cycle, sometimes there's a gap between what we think we're doing and what we're actually doing. For example, many executives and entrepreneurs routinely tell people they work eighty to one hundred hours a week. The truth is probably somewhere closer to sixty. We deceive ourselves so easily.

Especially in an environment of rapid change, it's easy to delude yourself about how you're spending your time and energy.

A time audit to figure out where your time is really going is a great way to get to the truth. There are digital and analog tools that will help you track how you spend your time, or you may want to simply write down in a notebook how you spent each hour and do the math manually. Whatever works best for you.

Similarly, make sure the hours you selected for your Green, Yellow, and Red Zones are still accurate. Did they shift a bit? Contract? Expand? Make sure that what was true is still true.

In addition, look at the demands on your time—often they will creep up without your realizing it, or the nature of the requests for your time will change, making it harder to say no. That could, of course, mean it's time to rethink your categories (something we covered in chapter 7) and figure out new ways to think through opportunities.

Growth, of course, is one among many challenges. Moving from employed to unemployed, dealing with a season of stagnation or decline in your company or industry, or any number of other changes can mean that what used to be effective for you isn't anymore.

When you find yourself in a place of unexpected change, work through these eight questions to help you diagnose the problem:

1. *What's taking my time that shouldn't be?*
2. *What do I need more time to work on?*
3. *What's wasting my time?*
4. *How are my zones changing?*
5. *Whom should I start meeting with?*
6. *Whom should I not be meeting with anymore?*
7. *What's changing in the nature of my inbound requests?*
8 *What categories do I need to rethink?*

These questions can help you quickly recalibrate your Thrive Calendar to adapt to your new circumstances.

DO THE MATH

A third practice you may want to consider happens gradually and involves rethinking three time allocations. These adjustments are helpful because as you live and lead longer, your priorities, personality, and preferences will continue to evolve. As a result, you may hit seasons when you can't put your finger on why your Thrive Cycle isn't working the way it used to. You just realize the effectiveness has diminished.

When that happens (and it does happen), I've found it helpful to review three key ratios that predict how well you'll thrive in the future.

The three calculations are

- the percentage of time you spend alone versus with people
- the percentage of time you spend in meetings
- the percentage of time you spend at home versus on the road

Calculating these three percentages will give you insight into how you best function. You likely have an ideal percentage for each, and as you exceed your limits, you'll find your stress level growing.

The idea is to figure out a rough percentage split for all three factors and then design your calendar according to how much time you'll ideally spend doing each. Let's explore each further.

Calculation 1: Time Alone Versus Time with People

If you look at how you spend all your time, regardless of which zone you're in (Green, Yellow, or Red), your time essentially divides into two categories: time spent alone and time spent with other people. The question is, How much time should you spend on each? The answer, I suggest, is whatever mix you need to thrive.

Extroverts, of course, generally refuel and gain energy by being with people. Throw them into a party, and they light up, genuinely enjoying the interaction with other people. On the way home, they think about how awesome it was. Put them alone in a room, though, and their battery drains quickly. They can't wait to get back with people.

Introverts, on the other hand, tend to refuel and gain energy by being alone. Put them in the same party, and they may wander off to the side, happy to be by themselves and hoping they can leave soon. Or they may look for the person they know best and spend the entire evening hanging out with him or her. But put them alone in a room, and they can feel their energy surge.

Any idea which one describes you better?

Because introversion and extroversion change with time, I've been on both ends of the spectrum, so I know what it feels like to gain energy from people and to find energy by myself.

I'm naturally wired as an extrovert, and until I was forty, I got energy like most extroverts do—from other people. Around age forty, though, I noticed a shift in how I refuel—I started craving time alone. Since I recovered from burnout, solitude has become more of an oasis for me.

If you get the time-with-people-versus-time-alone formula right, you may be able to extend your Green Zone. If I'm alone uninterrupted, my Green Zone can last up to five hours. If I'm in meetings, I'm fortunate to get three hours highly energized. If you're meeting with the wrong people in your Green Zone, the rest of the day can flip to Red almost instantly. There's no right or wrong here, just awareness. So how do you refuel?

It's that kind of observation and self-awareness that can help you far more than you may realize. Pay attention to how your interaction with other people affects your energy and your mood.

Obviously, we all need a mix of both. Loneliness and isolation corrode the souls of a lot of leaders. But all-people-all-the-time can also be deeply stressful. So, what's your ideal mix? These days, mine is about 60 percent alone and 40 percent with people. Five years ago, it was 70 percent by myself and 30 percent with people. Twenty years ago, it might have been 20 percent alone and 80 percent with people. It doesn't matter what your mix is nearly as much as it matters that you know your mix.

Here are five questions you can use to help you determine your mix:

1. *How do I feel after meeting with the "right" people?* (Note: Draining people are always draining. See chapter 9.)
2. *How many hours with people can I handle before I become tired?*
3. *How do I do my best work—solo or collaboratively?*
4. *How long can I be alone before I break the silence and reach out to other people?*
5. *When I'm working optimally, how much people contact does that involve?*

I realize there are no simple answers here, but asking these questions over a period of time can help you adjust your percentage. When you get the percentage close to optimal, you'll enjoy meeting with people *and* enjoy being alone.

So, what do you think your mix of alone time to people time is? 50/50? 80/20? 70/30? 30/70? The best answer is whatever mix makes you thrive. Once you discover it, adjust your Thrive Calendar accordingly.

Calculation 2: Time Spent in Meetings

If there's one complaint I hear from leaders, it's that they feel like they have way too many meetings. When a title like *Death by Meeting* continues to be a bestseller (thank you, Patrick Lencioni), you know that meetings bother more than a few of us.

While running better meetings can help you solve some of the problem, you may also find that there's a mathematical factor in play in meetings, similar to time spent alone versus time spent with people. Most of us have a maximum number of hours we can spend in meetings before they start to adversely affect us.

I produce my best work and enjoy my life the most when I spend about 40 percent of my work time in meetings and 60 percent of my time working solo or corresponding with others outside official meetings. I can stretch the amount of time spent in meetings to 50/50 as a compromise during busy seasons, but once I go above that for more than a week, I'm living at a pace that drains me.

Another way to think about it, particularly as more work moves virtual and we spend our days staring into cameras and screens, is whether there's simply a maximum number of meetings you can take in a week. As I shared earlier, my current meeting cap is fifteen. Once I exceed fifteen meetings in a week, I get tired, agitated, and far less productive.

Again, your number will be different. But take the time to figure out your ideal ratio and perhaps meeting cap, and adjust your Thrive Calendar accordingly.

In the real world, you're not always going to be able to stay at your ideal ratio or under your cap. But even knowing this can be helpful because it can alert you, your team, and even your family ahead of time that a particular week or month is going to be challenging, and you can prepare for that.

Here are three questions to help you discern your meeting ratio and cap:

1. *How many meetings a day can I handle before I become tired?*
2. *How many meetings a week can I take before I feel depleted?*

3. *How many meetings can I take before my work suffers and I have to stay late or come in early to get my most important tasks done on time?*

While you might not have the freedom to overhaul your meeting rhythm, any adjustments you can make to optimize your time spent in meetings is a step in the right direction.

Calculation 3: Time at Home Versus on the Road

Maybe you travel only once a year for vacation, and if so, slip on over to the next chapter, our final one together. But many people travel much more than that. Travel doesn't have to be exotic or involve airports. Maybe your car is your office, or you cover a region or go from store to store or handle the sales for five states. This has nothing to do with how far away or glamorous your travel is and everything to do with how often you're in a set location versus on the road. As soon as you start traveling overnight or missing breakfast and dinner at home because of travel, it becomes something you need to monitor if you want to thrive.

In the same way that you have an effective meeting cap, you probably also have a maximum amount of time you can be on the road before it becomes counterproductive.

I know leaders who don't mind being on the road two hundred days a year. I have other friends who flirted with a lot of travel earlier in their careers but decided that, for them to thrive, they wanted to be away from home only about a couple of weeks a year.

Again, there's no magic answer here, but there is *your* answer. If you're on the road, what's your ideal mix? When you factor in that almost any travel makes most of us tired, the following five questions can help you figure out your ratio. When your answer to all of them becomes no or not really, you're probably spending more than your ideal amount of time on the road. Scale back accordingly.

1. *When I think of my next trip, am I excited to be heading out on the road?*
2. *Am I able to get all my important work done despite my travel?*
3. *Am I able to keep up my current level of travel and lead my team well at the office?*
4. *Am I able to keep up my current level of travel and lead a meaningful and rich home life?*
5. *Can I travel at my current level and still be highly energized for the work I need to do?*

Sometimes you get surprised along the way. Having traveled extensively before COVID-19 closed borders in 2020, I would have answered yes to most of those questions. But being grounded for over a year showed me that I actually enjoy being home a lot more than I thought I would. In addition, I was able to be much more engaged with and available to my team. Based on what I learned from my involuntary grounding during COVID-19, I'm now doing much less traveling.

KEEP ADJUSTING

Your mix in all three categories will be unique to you, but knowing the conditions under which you flourish will make you better able to design your ideal calendar and thrive on.

The fun news is, all these tools and skills you're learning become more familiar and natural as time moves on. Soon they'll become as comfortable as a favorite sweater. Your team will also become accustomed to the new patterns and even get better at asking the right questions. They'll get better at saying no with you and for you. It's pretty routine now for my staff to tell me, "Your January is already at capacity. You can't take on anything else." I've gotten much better at realizing we all have limits, giving the team extra days off after a heavy season, and using the framework we've covered in the book to realize that our team is at capacity and it's time to hire new people—because asking my current team to do more would really push them into the Stress Spiral.

As an employer, you don't want perpetually stressed employees. People bring their whole selves to the job, and when they're thriving, so does your company. So the periodic adjustments and the regular conversations you have around these principles make everyone better and your organization better.

And now you know this, too—if for some reason you're not thriving, simply adjust.

You've learned an awful lot about how to live in a way today that will help you thrive tomorrow. But doing what you're best at when you're at your best has one final benefit we haven't talked about yet—possibly the best benefit of all. So let's go there next.

CHAPTER 11 IN A SNAP

- *Stress* is a good bad word. Our culture hates stress yet thrives on it. As a result, the pullback toward stress is almost gravitational. Stress is a badge of honor in the hamster-wheel life everybody's living.

- You can't hire or hope your way out of overwhelm. Instead, you need to lead yourself out of it.

- Your agility is the cap on your ability.

- If you anticipate, instigate. Doing something before change happens is the best way to be ready when change happens.

- Over time, adjust three key percentages that will help you thrive: the percentage of time spent alone versus with people, the percentage of time spent in meetings, and the percentage of time spent on the road versus at home.

- As an employer, you don't want perpetually stressed employees. People bring their whole selves to the job, and when they're thriving, so does your company.

predestination!

HELLO FROM THE FUTURE YOU

It's Not Just What You Accomplish; It's Who You're Becoming

> What our life amounts to, at least for those who reach
> full age, is largely, if not entirely, a matter of what we
> become within.
>
> —Dallas Willard

Well, you've done it! You've escaped the giant sucking vortex that's the Stress Spiral and learned how to stay out of it. You're living in a way today that will help you thrive tomorrow by doing what you're best at when you're at your best.

Your Energy Clock and Thrive Calendar are finely tuned as you move through your Green, Red, and Yellow Zones day in and day out. You have a much better sense of what you're best at, whom you should invest your time in, and how to say no (nicely) like a pro.

The dopamine hits and deep satisfaction will continue as you tuck your kids in every night, sleep sweetly yourself, get more done in less time at work, get that book written, launch that podcast, or train for that marathon as the weight slowly comes off. You'll join the growing list of people who are getting their lives and leadership back. Progress can be deeply motivating.

But there's another motivation, one that will keep you engaged not just for months or years but perhaps for your entire life. If you wonder whether the long obedience in the same direction—the regular adjustments, recalibrations, and perseverance necessary to make the Thrive Cycle a lifelong guide—is all worth it, I want you to imagine yourself not tomorrow or next month but years from now. Perhaps decades from now. Imagine the future you at fifty or sixty-five or eighty-five, if you can stretch your imagination that far.

I'm a decade and a half into my journey with the Thrive Cycle. It's not like I don't experience stress anymore. I do. But in greatly reduced measure compared with my thirties, when the damage of the Stress Spiral moved me into burnout. A decade and a half of embracing the strategies in this book have produced a much better work in me—not a finished work yet (we're all in process), but a work with which I'm much happier, and so are those around me. Being at your best is to some extent about what you accomplish, but to a much deeper extent, it's about creating the space you need to focus on who you're becoming. That's what motivated me to write this book—a vision of the future you years, even decades, down the road.

Many of the stress stories and hard moments that animate this book are drawn from my younger years, when I was new in leadership and my kids were young. So let me catch you up with my current situation.

I was recently driving down the highway with my youngest son, who's now in his midtwenties. As we headed south toward downtown Toronto, he asked me, "Dad, any idea why you disliked camping so much when we were kids?"

Fair question.

We used to camp a lot when the kids were younger because it was inexpensive and because my family *loved it*. Me, not so much. For years, I despised everything to do with camping. It was my least favorite form of vacation. What I disliked most about camping was how little control this control freak had over his surroundings. Despite being six feet two, I'm not very physical or handy. I'm not exactly sure how to chop wood. Putting up a tent is mysterious. I don't know how to tie up those sleeping bags that have shoelace straps, because the bag squirts out the side as soon as you tighten it. Most of all, the clean freak in me dislikes rain and mud. Every time we would go camping, it would rain. On our tent. In our tent. Under our tent. In my sleeping bag. Under the tarp where we were trying to eat dinner. On the firepit.

The last time I went camping with my family when my sons were young, it rained so hard I packed everyone into the car, left our stuff at the site for the bears to eat, threw a temper tantrum the average two-year-old would be proud of, and drove home in the dark, sulking the whole trip.

I disliked camping so much that I even framed it as a theological issue. If God created us to be intelligent enough to invent electricity and live indoors, isn't it unfaithful to go back into the woods?

Exactly.

So, that was the end of my camping career. Until recently.

In the meantime, my family never gave up on camping. They, understandably, just stopped inviting me. Now that my boys are in their twenties, they cracked open the question of whether I'd ever try camping again.

Recently my son and his girlfriend gave my wife, Toni, the gift of a weekend away camping with them for Mother's Day. As they planned the trip, I did something I never thought I'd do. I asked whether I could come too.

The motivation? A few uninterrupted days with my wife and grown kids is an attractive proposition, even if it involves some potential suffering for me.

My son, remembering well the low maturity level of his father in the wilderness, made a rule: "Dad, if you're coming, you can't complain. No matter what."

I accepted the challenge.

Camping in perfect conditions would lead to little complaining. What I had to prepare myself for were imperfect conditions. So for weeks I thought through what it would be like if it weren't sunny and warm.

Turns out that was a good idea.

The kind of camping my family does these days involves going way off the grid. No trailers. No power. No showers. No running water. You pack everything on your back and in a canoe, then paddle miles to find your site.

We had to paddle and portage (which involves carrying your canoe across land to reach the next body of water) five miles to reach our campsite. That's about a four-hour trek. Within fifteen minutes of paddling onto the first lake, we heard thunder. Minutes later, it started pouring. We pulled off to the shore and took cover under a not-too-tall tree while the thunder and lightning crashed around us, only to head back onto the lake after the thunderstorm pushed past. The lightning may have moved on, but the rain didn't. We were drenched.

The portages (there were three) were, shall we say, expert level. I'm not an expert. Off we trudged, carrying canoe and gear over rocks, stumps, roots, and mud to the next lake, until we got to the site where we set up camp.

Over the course of our three-day trek, we had one sunny day, but for the rest, it rained. One day trip we took got shortened because of six additional portages no one realized were longer and more challenging than they appeared on the map. When we finally left the park as scheduled, the rain returned on cue, and we paddled three and a half hours back to the car, soaked once again.

Guess what? I didn't complain.

Surprisingly, I enjoyed it.

In fact, I'm planning on going *again.*

So . . . what changed?

I did.

In the car that day, as I unpacked my previous disdain for camping, I told my son how ill-equipped I felt for life and leadership in my thirties, that despite all the success we were experiencing externally, I felt like I was falling apart internally. With tears in my eyes at times, I've told my boys how much I regret the anxious, upset, frustrated dad I was in moments when they were younger.

We talked about the changes in my life over the last fifteen years, how figuring out how to live at a more sustainable pace has left me in a much better frame of mind—a frame of mind I wished he had known when he was four.

Some people say they don't have regrets. Well, I do.

I can't get those early years back. But I can live differently moving forward. So, we talked about it . . . at length.

And as I sat there by the campfire, looking out at the lake and the stars, I was thankful. Thankful I could go with my family into a place I wouldn't choose and enjoy it.

Doing what I'm best at when I'm at my best has helped me become a better communicator. Understanding my zones has helped me get far more done in much less time and step into my purpose with joy and conviction.

In the end, who you're becoming is so much more important than what you're doing.

But all of that pales in comparison with the character shift that's happening. The much better marriage. The deeper relationships with my now-grown sons. The time I spend in prayer and Scripture every morning. The peace with who I am and whom I was made to be. The hobbies, friendships, and rest I enjoy every day.

In the end, who you're becoming is so much more important than what you're doing.

It's time you stepped into the future. You're going to love the person you meet.

CHAPTER 12 IN A SNAP

- Doing what you're best at when you're at your best is the best way to escape the Stress Spiral and live in a way today that will help you thrive tomorrow.

- The dopamine hits that progress generates are motivating, but character formation and growth are more deeply motivating.

- Doing what you're best at when you're at your best is to some extent about what you accomplish, but to a much deeper extent, it's about creating the space you need to focus on who you're becoming.

- Who you're becoming is so much more important than what you're doing.

ACKNOWLEDGMENTS

Ah, where to start?

This book took a little more work and editing than any I've written so far. Okay, make that *a lot* more work and editing than any previous book. But when you apply the principles I've shared with you, you have that kind of time, right? Three years of writing, rewriting, rethinking, and revising yet again have led to the finished product. *So* many people helped.

The first iteration of the concepts that became this book happened in 2015 when I spoke in Washington, DC, to Mark Batterson's staff. After the talk, Mark came up to me, and the first words out of his mouth were "Carey, that needs to be a book." (It's always a good idea to listen carefully when a multiple *New York Times* bestselling author suggests you write a book.) And now, Mark, here's the book.

Prior to writing *At Your Best,* I pioneered a beta version of these principles in an online course called The High Impact Leader. I've had the privilege of leading over three thousand leaders through that course. Many thanks to the numerous High Impact Leader alumni who have been so encouraging to me and my team. I love hearing what you're doing with your lives and leadership. Cheering for you!

My wife, Toni Nieuwhof, provided so much helpful guidance that I can't even begin to describe my gratitude. She read every word of every draft multiple times. She put up with me using up my Green, Yellow, and Red Zones to meet deadlines. And she did it while finishing her own book, launching a podcast, and doing the very hard work of continuing to be my best friend. I cherish you forever.

A few friends became not just readers but companions on this journey: Frank Bealer, Jeff Brodie, Sarah Piercy, and Ann Voskamp gave detailed and extensive feedback and encouragement in the darkest moments when finishing felt impossible.

So many people read all or part of the manuscript and helped make it better. Thanks to Ali Gentry, Rachel Bensen, Chris Heaslip, John Ortberg, Joel Manby, Josh Valler, Dusty Rubeck, Sean Morgan, Jeff Henderson, Rob Meeder, Mark Clark, Dillon Smith, Rich Birch, Gary Hurst, Cathan Bowler, and Brad Lomenick.

To the High Impact Leader alumni who gave their feedback, a deep thanks: James R. Batten, Josh Pezold, Jason Morgan, Cole Parrish, Cassius Rhue, Sarah Ralls, Jill Kemmer, Zach Zook, Chris Trethewey, Chris Denham, Nicci Birley, Vanessa Audia, Chris Veley, Brynn Attaway, and Ken Leonard.

Special thanks to Lysa TerKeurst and Shae Tate, who not only read various drafts but also provided deep insight on how to write a better book. Those days we spent together in Charlotte to kick off this project—and the dialogue since then—have shaped me for years to come. And, reader, if you want to get serious about writing better, apply for Lysa's COMPEL Training. It's top shelf.

My editor Eric Stanford consistently provided invaluable feedback and tough love exactly when I needed it. His gifting, skill set, and direction made this a far superior manuscript to anything I would have produced on my own.

Jon Acuff, thanks for all the listening and the insights on titling and angling the book. You are a master at what you do.

Thanks to my amazing team at Carey Nieuwhof Communications. Working with you is pure joy. Anita Hintz designed the graphics in this book and helped with many of the downloads. In addition to reading various drafts, Dillon Smith led the marketing on this book. And to Lauren Cardwell, Sam Nieuwhof, Sarah Piercy, Erin Ward, Carly Voinski, Jacquelyn Clark, and Holly Beth Singleton, who all put up with me and ran the company while I wrote, thank you. Special thanks also to Chris Lema, Toby Lyles, and Alejandro Reyes, who every week help us do what we do for leaders.

To Esther Fedorkevich and the team at the Fedd Agency, thanks for making this possible. Esther, thanks for the early encouragement to pursue this topic in book form.

Special thanks to Tina Constable and Campbell Wharton at Penguin Random House, who helped us land on a final title and continually expressed their belief in the book.

To Andrew Stoddard, Abby DeBenedittis, Kayla Fenstermaker, Kimberly Von Fange, Laura Barker, Brett Benson, Johanna Inwood, Chris Sigfrids, and the other good people at WaterBrook, I'm so grateful for the extra grace you gave this project. And look—we have a book!

My greatest fear in these acknowledgments is that because this book took three years to write and went through so many drafts and edits, I will forget some important people in the journey. If you're looking for your name and I missed it, I hope we can still be friends. Let's make some time to hang out. Apparently, we have it.

GLOSSARY

A brief reference guide to a few of the unique terms used in *At Your Best*.

Green Zone: The three to five hours each day when your energy is high, your mind is clear, your focus is sharp, and you find it easy to think and to imagine, to contribute and to create.

Yellow Zone: Those hours in a day when your energy and effectiveness are moderate. You're neither at your best nor at your worst. You're in the middle.

Red Zone: Those hours in a day when your energy is low, you struggle to pay attention, and you have a hard time producing *any* meaningful work.

Stress Spiral: The default mode of life for most people in which unfocused time, unleveraged energy, and hijacked priorities leave them feeling overwhelmed, overcommitted, and overworked.

Thrive Cycle: A virtuous loop in which focused time, leveraged energy, and realized priorities help people do what they're best at when they're at their best, which results in living in a way today that will help them thrive tomorrow.

Thrive Calendar: A calendar that reflects your predecisions about how to spend your work and personal time, expressed in repeating appointments with yourself, week after week, year after year.

NOTES

Introduction

1. Ryan Pendell, "Millennials Are Burning Out," Gallup, July 19, 2018, www.gallup.com/workplace/237377/millennials-burning.aspx.

Chapter 1: Build a Life You Don't Want to Escape From

1. Habib Yaribeygi et al., "The Impact of Stress on Body Function: A Review," *EXCLI Journal* 16 (2017): 1057, www.ncbi.nlm.nih.gov/pmc/articles/PMC5579396/pdf/EXCLI-16-1057.pdf.

2. "Stress Effects on the Body," American Psychological Association, November 1, 2018, www.apa.org/helpcenter/stress-body; Yaribeygi et al., "Impact of Stress."

Chapter 3: You Actually Do Have the Time

1. Greg McKeown, *Essentialism: The Disciplined Pursuit of Less* (New York: Crown Business, 2014), 31.

Chapter 4: Find Your Green Zone

1. Daniel H. Pink, *When: The Scientific Secrets of Perfect Timing* (New York: Riverhead Books, 2018), 28.

2. Claire Diaz-Ortiz, "Claire Diaz-Ortiz on How to Find Success on Social Media, the Early Days and Current Mood on Social, and Tips for Entrepreneurial Parents," interview Carey Nieuwhof, *The Carey Nieuwhof Leadership Podcast,* episode 324, February 26, 2020, https://careynieuwhof.com/episode324.

3. Cal Newport, *Deep Work: Rules for Focused Success in a Distracted World* (New York: Grand Central, 2016), 150. Newport cited the work of Anders Ericsson and his collaborators.

4. Pink, *When,* 53, 70–71. Many hospitals and operating rooms, having noted this tendency, have developed protocols to combat it, even creating vigilance breaks to refocus everyone, which is commendable. Still, if you can get the 9:00 a.m. appointment . . .

Chapter 5: Do What You're Best At

1. Thanks to Andy Stanley for that definition of *gifting.*

2. *Chariots of Fire,* directed by Hugh Hudson, Enigma Productions, Allied Stars, 1981.

3. Gary Keller's famous question "What's the ONE Thing I can do such that by doing it everything else will be easier or unnecessary?" is worth asking from time to time, too, particularly if you get stuck on what's most important. Gary Keller, *The ONE Thing: The Surprisingly Simple Truth Behind Extraordinary Results* (Austin: Bard, 2013), 112.

4. Malcolm Gladwell, *Outliers: The Story of Success* (New York: Little, Brown, 2008), chapter 2.

5. Seneca, *On the Shortness of Life* (c. AD 49), in *Dialogues and Letters* (London: Penguin Books, 1997), 69.

Chapter 6: Yellow Zone, Red Zone, and Other Real-Life Problems

1. Obviously, if you are a receptionist, work at a restaurant or in retail, or work with your hands, you might have all forty work hours prescribed by someone else. But that still leaves you with 128 hours every week. As Henry Cloud said in his book's subtitle, you are ridiculously in charge of your life. Henry Cloud, *Boundaries for Leaders: Results, Relationships, and Being Ridiculously in Charge* (New York: Harper Business, 2013).

2. For more on how to create a flexible workplace, see the resources I've created for employers and employees at www.LeadABetterTeam.com.

Chapter 7: Hijacked

1. Stephen R. Covey, *The 7 Habits of Highly Effective People: Powerful Lessons in Personal Change* (New York: Free Press, 2004), Habit 3.

2. Steve Jobs, *I, Steve: Steve Jobs in His Own Words*, ed. George Beahm (Evanston, IL: B2 Books, 2011), 43.

Chapter 8: Distraction-Free

1. Michael Winnick, "Putting a Finger on Our Phone Obsession," Dscout, June 16, 2016, https://blog.dscout.com/mobile-touches.

2. Nir Eyal, *Indistractable: How to Control Your Attention and Choose Your Life* (London: Bloomsbury, 2020), 12.

3. Herbert A. Simon, "Designing Organizations for an Information-Rich World," in M. Greenberger, ed., *Computers, Communications, and the Public Interest* (Baltimore: Johns Hopkins Press, 1971), 37–72.

4. Gloria Mark, "Worker, Interrupted: The Cost of Task Switching," interview by Kermit Pattison, Fast Company, July 28, 2008, www.fastcompany.com/944128/worker-interrupted-cost-task-switching.

5. Cal Newport, *Deep Work: Rules for Focused Success in a Distracted World* (New York: Grand Central, 2016), 6, 14.

6. Sarah Stodola, *Process: The Writing Lives of Great Authors* (New York: Amazon, 2015), 86. Special thanks to my editor Eric Stanford for this glorious fact about Nabokov.

7. If you're expecting an urgent text or phone call from someone who isn't programmed to break through the wall, just turn off Do Not Disturb for a short window, take the call, and then flip back to DND.

8. Friedrich Nietzsche, *Twilight of the Idols*, trans. Duncan Large (1889; repr., Oxford: Oxford University Press, 1998), 9.

9. Courtney Connley, "LeBron James Reveals the Nighttime Routine That Helps Him Perform 'at the Highest Level,'" CNBC, December 23, 2018, www.cnbc.com/2018/12/21/lebron-james-reveals-the-nighttime-routine-that-sets-him-up-for-success.html.

10. Rob Pelinka, "Rob Pelinka, L.A. Lakers' GM on Swimming with Great White Sharks with Kobe Bryant, Building a World Championship Team, and How Humility Can Transform Egos and Talent," interview by Carey Nieuwhof, *The Carey Nieuwhof Leadership Podcast*, episode 393, January 25, 2021, https://careynieuwhof.com/episode393.

Chapter 9: What About People?

1. John Townsend, *People Fuel: Fill Your Tank for Life, Love, and Leadership* (Grand Rapids, MI: Zondervan, 2019), 200.

2. An Enneagram Two, for example, would fit this description. See Ian Morgan Cron and Suzanne Stabile, *The Road Back to You: An Ennea-*

gram Journey to Self-Discovery (Downers Grove, IL: IVP Formatio, 2016).

3. Robin Dunbar, *How Many Friends Does One Person Need? Dunbar's Number and Other Evolutionary Quirks* (Cambridge, MA: Harvard University Press, 2010), 33.

4. Dunbar, *How Many Friends*, 24, 26–28, 32–33. Start to look for these numeric patterns, and you'll see them everywhere, from executive and leadership teams (three to ten), to sitcoms (the number of characters you can track with), to churches (the average congregation is under 150).

5. Dunbar, *How Many Friends*, 34.

6. Dunbar, *How Many Friends*, 21.

Chapter 10: The Big Sync

1. Ernest Hemingway, "Ernest Hemingway, The Art of Fiction No. 21," interview by George Plimpton, *Paris Review*, no. 18 (Spring 1958), www.theparisreview.org/interviews/4825/the-art-of -fiction-no-21-ernest-hemingway.

ABOUT THE AUTHOR

Carey Nieuwhof is a former lawyer, a bestselling leadership author, a podcaster, and the CEO of Carey Nieuwhof Communications.

Carey speaks to leaders around the world about leadership, change, and personal growth. He writes one of today's most widely read leadership blogs at www.CareyNieuwhof.com. He also hosts the top-rated *Carey Nieuwhof Leadership Podcast*, where he interviews some of today's best leaders. His content is accessed over 1.5 million times a month.

He and his wife, Toni, have been married for three decades and have two grown sons.

Reclaim 3 Productive Hours TODAY with the Free Thrive Calendar

THRIVE CALENDAR

	SUNDAY	MONDAY	TUESDAY	WEDNESDAY	THURSDAY	FRIDAY	SATURDAY
6:00AM – 7:00AM	Family and Personal Time	Personal Time	Personal Time	Personal Time	Personal Time	Personal Time	Family and Personal Time
8:00AM 9:00AM 10:00AM 11:00AM	Family and Personal Time	Writing	Strategy	Talk Preparation	Strategy	Writing	Family and Personal Time
12:00PM – 1:00PM		Short-Term Projects + Lunch	Calendar Management + Lunch	Meeting + Lunch	Meeting + Lunch	Strategy + Lunch	
2:00PM		Podcast Prep	Writing	Strategy	Writing	Projects	
3:00PM – 4:00PM		Podcast Interviews	Meetings + Admin	Podcast Interviews	Meetings + Admin	Planning + Admin	
5:00PM – 6:00PM		Exercise + Free Time	Meetings + Free Time	Exercise + Free Time	Admin + Free Time	Exercise + Free Time	

"Using this calendar template and the strategy behind it, I've personally been able to free up over 3 productive hours a day. That adds up to over 1,000 productive hours a year."
—CAREY NIEUWHOF

You can download the Thrive Calendar template and get a free training video series from Carey Nieuwhof by going to **AtYourBestToday.com**

WATERBROOK

Anticipate Your Obstacles.
Alter Your Outcomes.
Learn to See It Coming.

Nobody sets out to be cynical, disillusioned, or burned out,
but so many well-meaning leaders end up in exactly that place.

Any idea if that could happen to you?
Could it be happening to you right now,
and you're not even aware of it?

Learn to see the 7 issues that take out otherwise
great leaders in *Didn't See It Coming*.

You can learn more about the book at
DidntSeeItComingBook.com

WATERBROOK

Fascinating Conversations
with World-Class Leaders:
The Carey Nieuwhof Leadership Podcast

Ever wish you could have a conversation with today's top leaders in entrepreneurship, business, and leadership?

That's what this leadership podcast is designed to bring to you—backstage access to the people who lead extraordinarily well, such as Simon Sinek, Seth Godin, Nancy Duarte, Adam Grant, Cal Newport, Lysa TerKeurst, Craig Groeschel, Liz Forkin Bohannon, Michael Hyatt, Andy Stanley, and more.

All of it is designed to help you and your team thrive in life and leadership.

Subscribe for free on Spotify, Apple Podcasts, anywhere you listen to podcasts, or at
CareyNieuwhof.com/Podcast

WATERBROOK